THE CONVICTION OF
RICHARD NIXON

THE CONVICTION OF
RICHARD
NIXON

THE UNTOLD STORY OF THE
FROST/NIXON INTERVIEWS

JAMES RESTON, JR.

HARMONY BOOKS / NEW YORK

Published in the United States by Harmony Books, an imprint of the Crown
Publishing Group, a division of Random House, Inc., New York.

www.crownpublishing.com

Harmony Books is a registered trademark and the Harmony Books colophon is
a trademark of Random House, Inc.

Library of Congress Cataloging-in-Publication Data

Reston, James, 1941–

The conviction of Richard Nixon : the untold story of the Frost/Nixon
interviews / James Reston, Jr. – 1st ed.

1. Nixon, Richard M. (Richard Milhous), 1913–1994—Interviews.

2. Presidents—United States—Interviews.   3. Ex-presidents–United States—
Interviews.   4. United States—Politics and government—1969–1974.

5. Watergate Affair, 1972–1974.   6. Interviews—United States.   7. Frost,
David, 1939 Apr. 7–8. Reston, James, 1941–   I. Title.

E856.R47 2007

973.924092—dc22   2007001238

ISBN 978-0-307-39420-0

Printed in the United States of America

Design by Leonard W. Henderson, Jr.

10   9   8   7   6   5   4   3   2   1

First Edition

For

D. B. L. and M. L. R.
In '77 the gleam in my eye

Pick out the three best men you have in your fleet, and I will tell you all the tricks that the old man will play on you. The moment you see that he is asleep, seize him. Put forth all your strength and hold him fast, for he will do his very utmost to get away from you. He will turn himself into every kind of creature that goes upon the earth and will become also water and wondrous blazing fire. But you must hold him fast and grip him tighter and tighter, until he begins to talk to you. When at length of his own will he speaks, then, hero, stay thy might, and set the old man free.

The Odyssey,

BOOK IV

FOREWORD

"If the President does it, that means it's not illegal."

Those brazen words, uttered by Richard Nixon in his famous interview with David Frost in 1977, come eerily down to us through the tunnel of the last thirty years. In the area of criminal activity, Nixon argued, the President is immune. He can eavesdrop; he can cover up; he can approve burglaries; he can bend government agencies like the CIA and the FBI to his own political purposes. He can do so in the name of "national security" and "executive privilege." And when these acts are exposed, he can call them "mistakes" or "stupid things" or "pipsqueak" matters. In the twenty-first century, Nixon's principle has been extended to authorizing torture, setting up secret prisons around the world, and ignoring the requirement for search warrants. A president can scrap the Geneva Convention and misuse the Defense Department and lie about the intelligence analyses. He is above the law. This is especially so when the nation is mired in an unpopular war, when the country is divided, when mass protests are in the streets of America, and an American president is pilloried around the world.

•   •   •

If Nixon's words resonate today, so also does the word *Water-gate*. Again the nation is in a failing, elective war. A Nixon successor is again charged with abuse of power in covering up and distorting crucial facts as he dragged the country, under false pretenses, into war. Again secrecy reigns in the White House, and the argument is made that national security trumps all. More than thirty years after the fact, the details of Watergate, in all its manifestations and with its bewildering cast of characters, may seem like a remote event in American political history. But in its essence, it was a signal turning point.

The power of the Frost/Nixon interviews, a milestone in media history and in the modern American presidency, remains undiminished. They raise the universal question of how a country comes to terms with an ugly episode in its recent past. They raise the question of how a leader who has abused his power is brought to justice once he is disgraced and removed from office, even if that justice is only moral or metaphysical. Sometimes it takes a showman with wit and courage to deliver that final chapter. In the case of the Frost/Nixon interviews, it took a showman who understood the power of the television close-up.

Watergate began small with a break-in at the offices of the Democratic National Committee at the Watergate Hotel in Washington on June 17, 1972. Five men were arrested: four Cubans and James McCord, a former FBI and CIA agent who was serving as the "security director" for the Committee to Reelect the President (CREEP). Across the street, armed with cameras and binoculars, were their co-conspirators and managers, E. Howard Hunt, a veteran CIA agent, and G. Gordon Liddy, a former FBI agent. These were the "Watergate Seven," the original burglars, the purpose of whose burglary was to discover incriminating political ammunition in the confidential files of the political opposition. From the outset, percolating down from the Oval Office itself through the offices of the West Wing and the Executive Office Building, a massive effort began to cover up the link between the break-in and the president's reelection campaign. Pressure was put on the original burglars to keep quiet; piles of "hush money" were paid to secure their silence. That cover-up lasted for nine months until its full scope was laid before Nixon in his conversation with White House counsel John Dean (who had been managing the cover-up) on March 21, 1973. That hour-and-a-half interchange was later referred to as the "cancer on the presidency" conversation.

In the spring of 1973 the focus shifted to the congressional investigations of the scandal. First came the Watergate hearings of the Senate Select Committee under Senator Sam Ervin, in which the principals were grilled and the secret Oval Office taping system was revealed. The matter moved into the courts when Nixon was forced to appoint a special prosecutor and the White House fought to block access to the damning evidence of the Oval Office tapes, using the spurious argument of executive privilege. Then came the House Impeachment Committee under Representative Peter Rodino. On July 24,

1974, in a case called *United States v. Nixon,* the White House lost its legal battle and was ordered to surrender the tapes to the special prosecutor. A week later, the smoking-gun tape of June 23, 1972, was made public, and four days after that, Richard Nixon resigned.

In the two years of this spasm in American political life, the definition of Watergate had grown and broadened from a break-in and cover-up to a broad pattern of abuse and obstruction of justice. Yet, with Nixon's resignation on August 9, 1974, the country was left with unfinished business. The man at the center of the conspiracy, the President of the United States, was left in splendid Napoleonic isolation in a place called San Clemente, California. True, he was driven from office. Three articles of impeachment, on obstruction of justice, on abuse of power, and on contempt of congress, were voted out of committee to the floor of the U.S. House of Representatives. After the revelation of the June 23 tape, Nixon's support evaporated in both the House and the U.S. Senate. His impeachment in the House and eventual conviction in the Senate were certain.

But then he resigned, and shortly afterward he was pardoned by his successor, Gerald Ford, of any real or supposed crime. In the months following his resignation, one top White House official after another went to jail for perjury, obstruction of justice, and illegal campaign activities: H. R. Haldeman, John Ehrlichman, John Dean, John Mitchell, Herbert Kalmbach, and Nixon's henchman, Charles Colson. Though the grand jury named him an "unindicted co-conspirator," Nixon avoided testimony in a court of law, most pointedly in the Watergate trial of his chief of staff, H. R. Haldeman, because he had suffered an attack of phlebitis, and his doctors said he was too sick to testify. The ex-president recovered nicely after the trial was over.

Through it all, Nixon remained a combative figure, disgraced but uncontrite and unconvicted. He seemed to feel that with time the odor of scandal would pass, and somehow he would be vindicated. History would remember his great accomplishments, he proclaimed, like the opening to China and the winding down of the Vietnam War—the "big things" as he called them—and forget this "pipsqueak thing" called Watergate. He fell back on the essential spirit of the U.S. justice system that presumes innocence until guilt is proven. Since the House of Representatives as a full body had not voted impeachment and the U.S. Senate had not tried and convicted him, he insisted on his innocence. His full defense had never really been tested, at least not with the chief conspirator in the dock. Someday he would stride proudly again on the world stage as an elder statesman, whose wise counsel was sought by kings and potentates.

Then, in 1976, two years after his resignation, he made a lucrative and exclusive arrangement with David Frost, the English entertainer, to submit to more than twenty hours of questioning on all aspects of his presidency. The show on Watergate would be the centerpiece.

. . .

In 1976, when David Frost asked me to help him prepare for the Watergate interrogation of Nixon, I was living on my farm outside Chapel Hill, North Carolina, toiling on a faltering novel, teaching creative writing at the university, and enjoying life in the piney woods. The lure was irresistible. The Frost/ Nixon interviews would include the only trial over Watergate that Nixon would ever endure. It would be a trial on television, part history, part show business, part inquisitional sport, and I was invited into the center of this unprecedented enterprise. Their outcome was uncertain. The interviews could result in the vindication of the nation's decision: the conviction of Richard Nixon. That was an outcome the nation would demand, and what I demanded as the price of my involvement. Or they could be his exoneration at the hands of a lightweight. If it was the latter, Nixon's reputation might be rehabilitated, a result that made me cringe, especially so because Frost was paying Nixon over a million dollars for this privilege. Inevitably, the decision of the nation would be questioned. And so the project was freighted with enormous historical significance. As the reputations of Nixon and Frost were on the line, so, too, were the reputations of the secondary players, including myself. I felt the weight of our historic responsibility intensely.

In running a criminal conspiracy out of the Oval Office, Nixon dragged the country through two years of agony over his Watergate transgressions. His abuses of his presidential office, his obstruction of justice, his cover-up, his plans for break-ins and wiretapping, his program for political spying and sabotage had become perfectly clear to the American people in court trials and in congressional inquiries. Just as he was on the verge of being impeached by the U.S. House of Representatives and then tried and formally removed from office by the U.S. Senate for high crimes and misdemeanors—the only president in American history to suffer such a fate—he had abruptly resigned. Gerald Ford's pardon ensured that the disgraced president would never stand before the bar of justice.

"Our long national nightmare is over," Ford had proclaimed when he took office. But it was not over, it could not be ended simply by waving the wand of pardon and wishing the demons to go away. The crimes needed to be defined and addressed and acknowledged, so they could be digested and remembered before they could be consigned to the bin of history. If they were properly remembered in the decades to come, Watergate crimes might not be repeated.

*   *   *

Richard Milhous Nixon was the last of the political giants in twentieth-century American politics. Over nearly thirty years in the public eye, his skill in statecraft and in political witchcraft were transcendent. If he was associated with dirty tricks and sleazy politics, he had also won two presidential elections. No one ever suggested that Richard Nixon was a fool. As president, his accomplishments were undeniable: the opening to China, the painful drawing-down of the Vietnam War, his brinksmanship in the nuclear age. With his partner, Henry Kissinger, his successes in Middle East and Cold War politics were considerable, as were his achievements with another partner, Daniel Patrick Moynihan, in the domestic arena.

Our task was daunting. From the beginning of my involvement, I thought of Nixon as Proteus. This mythological Greek god of the sea possessed all the wizardlike wiles: he was well protected by guards and well endowed with cunning. When he was threatened or cornered, he could miraculously change shape and voice in order to effect his escape. Again and again I returned to Book IV of *The Odyssey,* in which the difficulty of snaring Proteus was described. The Old Man of the Sea, as the watery god was called, would emerge warily from the brine, carrying with him the fishlike stench of the deep. To capture Proteus, Odysseus would have to summon all his strength and courage. He would need Olympian exertions from his three most stalwart oarsmen. If Odysseus was lucky enough to grab the old sorcerer, he must hold on bravely as the beast changed from a lion with a great mane into a dragon and a wild boar, then into running water and blazing fire, and finally into a tree. Odysseus must grip his quarry ever more tightly as Proteus struggled and shifted shape, until finally the god of the deep tired, and then he would begin to talk freely and honestly. In David Frost, we had a most unlikely Odysseus.

Indeed, the project did have elements of Greek theater. Two fading figures were trying to use each other to revive their shrinking standing in the world. It was single combat in the medieval sense, and only one of them could prevail. Glory or disgrace, their fate was their own to grasp. There could be no such thing as a draw. Nixon had his enemies list, but he was his own worst enemy; that was his vulnerability. Frost had spent his career largely in satirical comedy and entertainment and soft-soap celebrity interviewing. His strength was his wit. And yet the challenge was deadly serious. In the fine tradition of Aeschylus, their character was their destiny.

Undoubtedly, Nixon saw the enterprise as a sweetheart deal. He stood to make a lot of money and to rehabilitate his reputation in the bargain. Through Frost, he surely hoped to show that the nation had made a mistake. Perhaps he was dreaming about yet another rise from the dead. Hundreds of prosecutors and newsmen had tried to corner him before, and had failed. How could this show, especially with this lightweight showman, be any different? But Nixon underestimated the great skill of his interlocutor and the power of the research behind him. And the ex-president disregarded the power of television, especially the power of the television close-up. If Nixon's advantage was his experience and his gravitas, Frost's advantage was his understanding of the camera's unflinching eye.

As time drew close to the broadcasts, the public, too, was skeptical that anything of significance would emerge from the interviews. Indeed, a whiff of a secret deal between the players was in the air—a fix. "The Frost/Nixon sessions represent another typical Nixon deal," wrote the TV columnist of the *Chicago Tribune*. "The deck is stacked, and the cards are marked."

This bout of heavyweights remains the most-watched public affairs program in the history of television. More than 45 million people tuned in. Seated on their boxers' stage in coastal California, the contenders appeared on the covers of *Time* and *Newsweek*. Over the four days of their initial broadcast, the *New York Times* carried its news accounts on its front page, the transcript of the exchanges on its inside pages, and its running commentary in its editorials. Who would win? Was the Englishman up to the job? Would there be revelations or just rehashes? Would it be exciting or boring? But, most important of all, would Nixon confess to his crimes? Or would he make his actions out to be benign and all too human? If he confessed, would he apologize? And if he apologized to the nation, would it be an authentic apology, or just another scripted piece of Nixonian fakery? Was Nixon a dead duck? Or had he put another one over on us?

The Conviction of Richard Nixon is the account of my involvement in the Nixon interviews as David Frost's Watergate adviser. I wrote it in the summer and fall of 1977 when I had returned to North Carolina and to university life. And then I put it away for thirty years, until I fished it out once again and gave it to the playwright Peter Morgan, as grist for his play *Frost/Nixon*.

On the thirtieth anniversary of this famous television event, this book finally answers the question, often put to me over the years, of how Frost "did it." How did this English-man bring this formidable figure of twentieth-century American politics to say, in an apparent personal epiphany, "I have impeached myself"?

James Reston, Jr.
Fiery Run, Virginia

PART I

Washington

THE INVITATION CAME in a curious, roundabout fashion. Joseph Kraft, the syndicated Washington columnist who was acting as David Frost's recruiter, encountered my mother at a less-than-intimate Washington party and casually wondered where that son of hers was—whether Richard, James, or Thomas, he was not sure—who had worked with Frank Mankiewicz on a Watergate book several years ago. He was back in North Carolina, she replied, had just finished a book on the Joan Little case, and was teaching creative writing. Do you suppose, Kraft wondered, that he would be interested in working with David Frost on the Nixon interviews? Mom was discreet, as always. She would ask.

David Frost? I knew he was British. I had vaguely pleasant memories of *That Was the Week That Was* (*TW3,* I later learned to say), quite brilliant satire and political humor that was my style ("birth control: booby prize of the week" was an example). Hadn't there been an interview show later? I thought I remembered a sensitive interview with Jimmy Webb, one of my favorite singers, after "By the Time I Get to Phoenix," but it might have been Merv Griffin. I couldn't be sure. Clearly, I needed to find out more.

Sure enough, Frost had had an interview show; he had even once offered my father $10,000 to appear on his show for ninety minutes, but Dad had turned the offer down. In 1968 Frost had interviewed all the presidential candidates, including Richard Nixon. From James David Barber, the political scientist at nearby Duke University, I discovered that Frost had asked questions of Nixon like "Are there any essentially American characteristics?" and "For an American today, what can the dream or goal be?" and (perhaps best of all) "This is a vast question, I know, but at root, what would you say that people are on earth for?"

Work with David Frost on the Nixon interviews? He wouldn't need much help to devise questions like those. But Barber cautioned against cynicism. The responses from Nixon to Frost's grandiose offerings had been revealing, both in political and personal terms. Barber had quoted copiously from them in his acclaimed *Presidential Character*. Frost was, Barber felt, a subtle and clever interviewer, probably better than anyone we had on the American scene to interview a slippery Nixon.

So I headed for New York and Frost's somewhat seedy offices in the Plaza Hotel. I had to wait for a time to see him. When I was ushered in, Frost apologized profusely for the delay; he had finally gotten through to the South of France after trying for four hours. I nodded as if I understood his frustration. At first we discussed his bona fides rather than mine. Expressed in polite language, I had three questions: Why, I asked, could he do any better than, say, Dan Rather or Mike Wallace? In the back of my mind was Wallace's boorish failure in interrogating H. R. Haldeman. It had been one of the outrages of modern television; Haldeman had reportedly received $100,000 for his time, and nothing of interest had come from the interview. What was the argument for paying Nixon so much money? (The scandal sheet *The National Enquirer* was reporting that week that Nixon would make $650,000 for the interviews. It was much more, I learned later.) And would Frost feel a certain awe or respect in Nixon's presence, so characteristic of American newspeople, or was he prepared to go for the jugular?

Frost was an amiable good sport. We drank warm champagne, and he offered me an expensive cigar in a plastic case. (Later, during the interviews, Nixon would say to me, "David Frost always goes first class. What are you having for lunch today—duck under glass?") He had interviewed many world leaders since 1967, Frost asserted, and had earned his reputation in Britain as a withering interrogator. Playing to my novelist's sensibility, he said he had never written a novel, but he was interested in what made Richard Nixon tick. Nixon was the most interesting man in the world to interview. And Frost did indeed share my sense of historical responsibility: to be the only man who would ever question Nixon at length about his Watergate involvement was a daunting challenge.

Frost's ordinariness and honesty and good humor impressed me. He was slightly plumper than I imagined. His face certainly was not the reason for his success, and he possessed a high-pitched, loud laugh that tended toward grating. He had a curious mannerism of crooking his fingers in front of him when he made a point, as if he were reaching for two safe dials. I was astonished to find out later that only two years separated us in age. He was thirty-eight, but he looked older.

In 1975 he had been nominated to be knighted, but someone within the nominating committee had been so scandalized at the idea of such a middlebrow as a knight of the Queen that he leaked the nominations to the press. It was the first time in history that had ever happened. The uproar over Frost was so intense that his name was withdrawn.

The trip to New York was something of a lark for me. I couldn't imagine that this entertainer was really serious about wanting a first-rate team of researchers and advisers. The interviews had the feel of show business rather than journalism. Whatever Frost's reputation may once upon a time have been in Britain, it had not kept when he crossed the Atlantic. I had already heard the rumors that Frost had been chosen by Nixon because the disgraced president saw the Englishman as a soft touch. From the personal point of view, it was hard to imagine that Frost would meet my demands: I would have to take a leave of absence from the University of North Carolina and move to Washington for six months. My price was high. But to my astonishment, three weeks later I found myself in a plush apartment in Georgetown, the details all worked out, and work on Watergate under way.

· · ·

Because I come from a journalistic family and know the incestuous, parasitic relationship between Washington newsmen and men of power, I was anxious to get guidance from friends in the academic community about the highest value that the Frost/Nixon interviews might attain, before I immersed myself in the Washington maelstrom. So in early July 1976, the week before I left for Washington, I gathered together an eclectic group of academics to discuss the project. The group included a law dean, a psychiatrist, a philosopher, and a novelist, along with the obligatory political scientist and historian. The participants expressed general skepticism that Nixon would say anything different from his previous utterances on Watergate if the interviews followed traditional lines. They had high regard for Nixon as a master weasel, and if the Watergate interview was treated as the interrogation of a hostile witness, they held little hope for a fruitful exchange. The law dean cited the deposition of Nixon in the Halperin wiretap case, conducted by a friend of his, where Nixon had bested the Halperin lawyers with skill and condescension. At one point in the deposition, Nixon had sounded huffy in the words he spoke for the record, but had winked at his interrogator. To prove Nixon a liar, the group felt, was to prove an a priori proposition. As a lawyer and a politician, he would have a refined sense of how to parry hostile questions. In the position of adversary, he was bound to win—and if the result of a Frost adversarial stance was to elicit nothing new, the American public would be utterly outraged. The higher star to shoot for, said James David Barber, would be an answer to the question: How was it possible that a man like this was able to exploit the American political system as he did, from the Checkers Speech forward? The viewers, Barber felt, should come away with a sense of the vulnerabilities of the American political system. To accomplish this, the shows should aim to expose this complicated and banal and anti-democratic personality who nearly did in the American system.

We should hold the details of Watergate until last, Dr. Barber advised, keeping Nixon on human ground in the beginning, where he was bound to be uncomfortable. We should confront him with human warmth and sympathy and humor, to which he would be unable to respond. Presenting Nixon with human material in an opening gambit would "detoxify" the interviews, the psychiatrist stated. Once into specific substantive areas, the tactics should be to ask general, conceptual questions like "What do you think the role of compromise is in political life?" or "How would you advise a young politician to deal with the press?" We should encourage Nixon to grandstand in his customary fashion. Once a general Nixonism was elicited, Frost could compare it to the specific facts of the Nixon record. Frost should play to Nixon's fascinations and motivations and sensitivities—say his fascination for the technique of politics. Frost might show him clips from his past performances, Checkers or the Farewell Address or a Vietnam speech, and ask him to comment on how well, in retrospect, he thought he had done, or how he might have handled the situation better or differently. And Frost should play to Nixon's sensitivity about how "history" would treat this or that event, remembering the anecdote from the tearful Kissinger session in the final days, in which the president blubbered, "Will history treat me more kindly than my contemporaries?" In psychiatric terms, said the psychiatrist, Nixon now was basically a dead person for whom involvement in politics, his reason for living, was over, and whose only remaining passion was how history would treat him. Fawn Brodie, the biographer of Nixon, later expressed this same thought somewhat differently—of the Nixon Memoirs, and implicitly the Frost electronic memoirs, Brodie wrote to me, "The most he [Nixon] can hope for from the new autobiography is to avoid being described by historians as the worst President in our history."

From this group discussion in Chapel Hill, I arrived in Washington with a strong bias against a facts-and-dates approach to the Nixon interview. This soon got me into considerable hot water, partly from the bias and partly from my own naïveté, and nearly resulted in my being fired before we even began.

In early July 1976, the first meeting of the Frost team took place in a style to which I soon became accustomed. David Frost flew in from London on the Concorde for a four-hour meeting, and then flew to New York for the night. He was accompanied by his chosen producer for the Nixon interviews, John Birt. Frost described him as "the most brilliant producer in Britain." John Birt's credentials were impressive. Only thirty-one, he had been a top public-affairs producer for ten years at ITV, the alternative network to the BBC, where he had produced the highly successful potpourri *Weekend World*. (Later he was appointed the director of the BBC.) A large, fleshy man with round, wire-framed glasses and the classic English cameo complexion, and in his speech, with a clipped, precise Oxfordian delivery, he was gray-haired already. Once I challenged him to a chess game. "I never play chess," he replied. "My whole professional career is a chess game."

We were joined in Birt's suite at the Madison Hotel by C. Robert Zelnick. Affable Bob hailed from the Bronx and had made his way to being bureau chief at National Public Radio by way of law school and the *Anchorage Daily News*. His tough-guy demeanor seemed cut out of his stint in the Marines, to which he often made reference; in time I learned his hitch had been for six months in the reserves, compared with my three years in the U.S. Army. Zelnick had been hired to handle the foreign policy and domestic policy segments, and was joining Frost after resigning from NPR in a news policy dispute. Zelnick was the made-to-order Washington newsman, in my over-easy construction of that exotic creature: well informed, experienced, and constantly referring to people in high places by their nicknames (Henry this, Jim Schlesinger that). I could see from the beginning that tension would develop between us.

So long had it been since I was employed by someone—in

my teaching and writing for eight years I had become accustomed to total independence—I was oblivious to the need for a prudent period of feeling-out. When David asked about possible approaches to the Watergate program, I came forward with the definitive opinions bred of the collaboration with Mankiewicz and nurtured by my Ivory Tower friends. Nobody remembered the important dates of Watergate, I asserted breezily. We must come up with a thematic approach, defining large philosophical themes to be explored in detail. I yawned figuratively when Zelnick talked about interrogating Nixon on revenue sharing or welfare reforms. Unless there was an edge and tension to the entire twenty-four hours of interview taping, the American people would be scandalized, I argued. Frost and Birt listened alertly as I dug myself in deeper and deeper. Zelnick was characteristically yeomanlike in his presentation on topics to be covered in his "areas."

The next day Birt tried to have me fired. He lectured me on what was "journalistic," and I countered that I did not need the lecture. He expressed great interest in Nixon's economics, calling himself a Keynesian, and I said Nixon's economics were hardly the passion of the American people at this point in history. We matched each other, arrogance to arrogance, my University College to his St. Catherine's (our Oxford colleges), but behind our conflict lay the question of authority. Could I be controlled? Even if I disagreed with the facts-and-dates approach, would I be willing to do this preliminary slogging back over the Watergate terrain? Birt suggested a two-week trial period. Out of the question, I countered. I had already found a replacement for my courses at the university. In an effort to retreat behind legality, I pointed to the verbal contract between David and myself. Soon enough, David made his decision. I would add something special to the team, he told Birt, a little passion perhaps. I would stay.

Birt flew back to London, unhappy that he had not succeeded in sacking me from the team, but confident that he had established his leadership. My suggestion of a thematic approach to Watergate had flopped. I accepted the verdict and began to immerse myself in the debris of the Watergate cover-up. Behind all this was Frost's perception of the show and of himself. He was growing into his role of inquisitor. He was confident in factual questioning but insecure with conceptual matters, and later this was dramatically demonstrated. Thus, given our "star," their emphasis on facts was the right one.

·   ·   ·

In the two months that followed, the forty-seven volumes of House Impeachment Committee evidence became my primary source, along with the 12,000 pages of testimony in the Watergate cover-up trial. It was tedious and depressing work. In the first two weeks of reacquaintance with the sleaziness and banality of it all, I was overcome with nausea and wondered what I had got myself into. Two years of Watergate is enough, Nixon had once said, and I was moving into my third year. But then I hit my stride, and the old fascinations, shared by so many Americans, began to return.

The main question became how Nixon could be questioned productively on the facts of the cover-up, when there were so many of them. My early approach was to define those major areas where Nixon, the presidential conspirator, had reportedly had direct criminal involvement. These were soon proscribed as six incidents from June 17, 1972, to April 30, 1973, when H. R. Haldeman, John Ehrlichman, John Dean, and Richard Kleindienst left the Administration:

1. The eighteen-and-a-half-minute gap on the June 20, 1972, tape. Haldeman's notes indicated that he and Nixon had discussed Watergate on this first working day back at the White House. The notes talked of a "PR offensive to top this" and "the need to be on the attack—for diversion." The evidence indicated that only three people could have caused the erasure: Stephen Bull, the presidential assistant; Rose Mary Woods, the President's secretary; or the President himself.

2. The June 23, 1972, smoking-gun tape. The disclosure of the three conversations with H. R. Haldeman on this day led a few days later to Nixon's resignation. The strategy for the CIA to block the FBI's investigation of

Mexican checks found in the bank account of Bernard Barker, one of the burglars, was devised by Haldeman and Nixon in these talks. This was a clear obstruction of justice. What could Nixon's defense to this definitive evidence be two years later?

3. The payment of "hush money" to the Watergate burglars. This process commenced on June 28, 1972, eleven days after the break-in, and was handled by Herbert Kalmbach, Nixon's personal attorney. In the three months that followed, Kalmbach had distributed $187,000; thereafter the distribution was managed by Fred LaRue, an assistant to John Mitchell, the head of the Republican presidential campaign. LaRue distributed another $230,000. Nixon had said that he didn't know this was going on until March of the following year, when White House counsel John Dean told him. But the use of Kalmbach eleven days after the break-in provided a strong circumstantial case that Nixon must have known about the process from the beginning. Had the President's lawyer been caught at this task, it would have associated the President with the break-in in the summer of 1972, and no one but Nixon would logically have authorized such a risky procedure.

4. Offers of clemency to Howard Hunt, January–March 1973. Only the President had the power to offer clemency, and the veiled threats of Howard Hunt, the leader of the burglars, to go public with his knowledge of the "seamy" things he had performed for the White House

extended back to November 1972. Only with money and the offer of a short prison term could he be persuaded to remain silent.

5. Payment of Hunt's blackmail demand of $120,000 on March 21, 1973. Hunt was paid that amount after several Nixon conversations that day with Dean, Haldeman, and Ehrlichman.

6. The offer of $200,000 to $300,000 for legal expenses to Haldeman and Ehrlichman on April 17 and 25, immediately before their resignation. Both aides refused the offer, but where would Nixon get that kind of cash? Was this the famous $100,000 of Howard Hughes's in Bebe Rebozo's account? Did Nixon have other monies lying around? That whole misty area had never really been touched.

By an intense interrogation of Nixon on these six areas alone, Frost could establish the President as a criminal—if that was to be Frost's ultimate goal.

In the summer of 1976, David Frost was as affected as everyone else by Bob Woodward and Carl Bernstein's influence on American journalism. He hoped devoutly that his Washington cadre—Reston, Zelnick, and later, for a short time, Washington freelancer Phil Stanford—would come up with a scoop or two. In my case, I was plowing over ground that had been covered by hundreds of journalists in Washington for two years, by the congressional committees of Senator

Sam Ervin and Congressman Peter Rodino with their power of subpoena, and by the Watergate Special Prosecutor's Office. Were Watergate scoops really a practical goal? I thought not.

In November 1976, Phil Stanford, our team member charged with researching all non-Watergate Nixon tricks (the Hughes connection, the Ellsberg break-in, the abuse of the CIA and other federal agencies, and the like), arranged for an interview with Charles Colson. I asked if I could tag along. For me, Colson occupied a special place of contempt among the Nixon convicts, and the source of the feeling lay in Vietnam rather than Watergate. For four years, in writing more than any other American writer about the issue, I had been a passionate advocate of amnesty for the resisters to America's longest immoral war. At the time when the public news was the return of American POWs and the controversy over amnesty (and the inside news was Nixon and Company orchestrating the Watergate cover-up), Colson had said about Vietnam war resisters:

> The pathetic impertinence of arguing that those who deserted or dodged the draft did so because they were endowed with some moral sensitivity denied to the rest of us would scarcely seem worth addressing at all. It is, however, on precisely this point that we begin to see the pernicious influence of those who have victimized impressionable young men. . . . However these young

men have been misled, it remains President Nixon's duty to treat them according to law. In truth, the last ten years was a time of fashionable expatriation, and it is not surprising that some young men felt they could have a soft life abroad while avoiding obligations at home. They are not, as some have said, victims of war—rather they are victims of their own character deficiencies and of those politicians who tragically exploited them.

By 1976, Colson's own character deficiencies were well known to most, even though he was skillfully and lucratively trying to mask them with his witness to Jesus. By the fall of 1976 he had made more money off Watergate than any other Nixon underling, including John Dean.

When Stanford and I arrived at his "Reconciliation House" in the posh Cleveland Park section of Washington, we were ushered into a beautifully appointed room full of antiques, bronze statuettes, leatherbound books. The room had the air of an executive suite. If one had to give over his life in sacrifice for Christ, this was certainly the way to go. Colson's secretary, a cheery, gullible woman, announced that "Chuck" would be down in a minute—some delay with respect to a German television production on "Religion in America." Chuck arrived after a time, his moon face, his glasses down his nose and slightly askew, his pouty, infant's lips just as they looked in his pictures. His secretary stayed and took notes on our conversation.

Stanford plied Colson with a number of questions about the enemies list, Teamster activities, miscellaneous abuses, while I remained dutifully quiet. Curiously, to demonstrate some point or another, Colson mentioned transcripts of conversations with Nixon that he had from the Watergate prosecution. Colson/Nixon conversations? My ears perked up. I had never heard of any. There were none in the Judiciary documents I was working with, nor in the edited transcripts released by Nixon. Of that much I was sure. I knew that Colson was a special crony of Nixon. Around town he was known as the master of Dirty Tricks. I also knew that in the darkest days of the cover-up for the Chief Conspirator (January–April 1973), Nixon would often call Colson as the last call of the night. Talking trench politics with Chuck was apparently sleep-inducing for Richard Nixon. Colson/Nixon conversations could be gold.

Trying to control my excitement and without much fanfare, I said, "Given the fact that you've made a full breast of your involvements, you wouldn't mind letting me see the transcripts of those Nixon conversations . . . ?" To my utter astonishment, he said, "Sure, come back in a week."

At the appointed time I returned to the Reconciliation House, and was greeted once again by Margaret Shannon, Chuck's secretary. Before she gave me the conversations, I asked her if she was sure of Colson's total commitment to

Christ. If she had any doubts, she said sweetly and earnestly, she would not work for him. Along the way in our chatting, as if to underscore the importance of her role, she let slip that San Clemente had been very concerned about some of the questions we'd asked Colson the week before. So that was it! Colson had seen us to judge our competence and to pass on our concerns to the Nixon people. The old network still worked. This would be a valuable lesson.

Miss Margaret sat me down at one of the French provincial tables, and laid the transcripts of five conversations in front of me: June 20, 1972; January 8, 1973; February 13, 1973; February 14, 1973; and April 12, 1973.

June 20, 1972! That was only three days after the Watergate break-in, on the same day that Nixon and Haldeman had talked about Watergate, and the tape had turned up with an eighteen-and-a-half-minute gap. If there was a conspiratorial conversation that same day with Colson, it would make the famous gap moot! Nixon's joining of the conspiracy at the very outset could be established through Colson rather than Haldeman.

But the excerpts were curiously bland and almost irrelevant. The June 20 portion contained only four interchanges, which had nothing whatever to do with Watergate and made no sense about anything that I could make out. The other exchanges were somewhat more pointed, but contained nothing startling. Chuck was busy on the day I read his transcripts, but I arranged to see him the following week. In the January 8 excerpts was a reference to an apparent dirty trick that Nixon and Colson were planning for Senator Birch Bayh of Indiana, something about planting a story about graft in his senatorial campaign. The idea, of course, was to get this story going about Bayh to divert attention from the Administration's Watergate problems. Before I saw Colson, I called Bayh's office and got the full context of the reference on the tape. I determined to use the reference as a litmus test for Colson's honesty and sincerity. When I saw him several days later, I asked where the rest of the June 20 conversation was.

"That was all the prosecutors gave us," he responded. What about the reference to Birch Bayh in the January 8 conversation? His face screwed up quizzically. He couldn't remember what that referred to; it had been three years.

He was lying. These were sanitized excerpts from the transcripts to give the appearance of being forthright, but conveying nothing damaging. What did I expect? I left hurriedly, not wanting to alert San Clemente any further about my interests. Now, at least, I knew what I was looking for.

Not long afterward, I was to spend several days at the Federal Court of Appeals, wading through the 15,000 pages of testimony in the Watergate cover-up trial. Of particular interest was the testimony of H. R. Haldeman in connection with two of the six areas of criminal conduct I had outlined for the interrogation of Nixon. Most important was Haldeman's lame explanation of the June 23, 1972, "smoking gun" conversation: he and Nixon were simply trying to protect a questionable campaign contribution by Nixon fund-raiser Kenneth Dahlberg, which had embarrassingly turned up in Bernard Barker's bank account. That was the "productive area" that the FBI investigation was then moving into in Mexico. Haldeman's explanation of the use of the CIA to block this FBI investigation was the only one on record of the June 23 tape, and gave us a clue to what Nixon would argue later. Second, Haldeman had been questioned about Nixon's personal offer of $200,000 in legal fees to him and Ehrlichman before their departure from the White House on April 30, 1973. Richard Ben-Veniste, the Watergate prosecutor, told the court: "The materiality of [Nixon's] offer was to show that they [Nixon, Haldeman, and Ehrlichman] were in it together and that the President would be willing to help them financially if they needed it. . . . It tended to show they all understood that they were protecting each other. This was part of the cover-up, and it was in this context that the offer was made." But, of course, only Nixon himself could answer the question of where his $200,000 in cash might come from.

In working at the Court of Appeals, plowing through the trial transcript pages, I was on familiar turf. Once before, in preparing to set a novel in the days of racial warfare in 1967 in Cincinnati, I had read with fascination the 2,000-page record of a murder/rape trial that had touched off the violence. I found the manner in which truth emerges in a trial—and judgment becomes possible—endlessly interesting. In the Cincinnati transcript there were, of course, the exhibits, and

I spent hours with them: the photographs of the crime scene, the lanyard embedded with beads that strangled the victim, the fingerprints of the defendant's clubbed fingers, taken from a doorknob. And so, when the marshal of the Court of Appeals took me back to the filing room to get the box full of transcripts for the cover-up trial, naturally I was also interested in the box next to it marked EXHIBITS.

When I got around to the exhibits (as an amusing break from the tedium of the public testimony), I found the usual goodies: a payment schedule of hush money by Howard Hunt's wife to the Cuban burglars; the altered day book of Jeb Stuart Magruder, a second-level conspirator; a floor diagram of the Democratic National Committee's offices in the Watergate building. And there also were transcripts of presidential conversations, dutifully filed in date sequence: Nixon/Colson, January 8, 1973; Nixon/Colson, February 13 and 14, 1973; Nixon/Colson, March 21, 1973. So here were full, unexpurgated conversations from which Colson himself had given me sanitized exchanges. Significantly absent, however, was the June 20, 1972, transcript I so coveted. There were other transcripts of interest, particularly a March 20, 1973, conversation with H. R. Haldeman. In my voracious devouring of these finds, I came across in the March 20 Haldeman conversation my favorite Nixon statement of all. He was talking about John Dean producing his phony "Dean Report," which would say no one in the White House was involved. The report, Nixon said, "should lay a few things to rest.

I didn't do this, I didn't do that, da-da, da-da, da-da, da-da, da-da, da-da, da-da, da. Haldeman didn't do this, Ehrlichman didn't do that. Colson didn't do that. See?"

Of the conversations I pulled from the record, the most significant were the February 13 and 14 Colson talks. Nixon's official position up through his resignation was that he had not learned about the Watergate cover-up until John Dean laid it all before him on March 21, 1973. And here he was discussing with Colson whether Mitchell would crack, how Hunt knew too much, how Magruder could limit the President's losses. Who was going to step forward and take the rap? So, within the transcript, six weeks before he had publicly said he knew anything about the cover-up, were these exchanges, the first on February 14:

> **N:** A cover-up is the main ingredient.
> **C:** That's the problem.
> **N:** That's where we gotta cut our losses. My losses are to be cut. The President's losses got to be cut on the cover-up deal.

And, even more important, on February 13:

> **N:** When I'm speaking about Watergate, though, that's the whole point, where this tremendous investigation rests. Unless one of the seven begins to talk. That's the problem.

In those exchanges alone, very good gangster talk indeed, there could not be more classic evidence of the president wriggling, maneuvering, scheming to escape the reach of the law. But since the Colson conversations were technically in the public record, I did not immediately perceive the significance of what I had unearthed. I assumed that these conversations had been released to the press, and were simply overlooked in the mounds of other released information.

In the late fall, when the gossip about Frost as a soft touch was rife, a Jack Anderson column about our project became extremely helpful. Under the headline DAVID FROST TO ASK TOUGH QUESTIONS, Frost was quoted as saying that if Nixon was not responsive to Watergate questions, his behavior would not be in the spirit of the contract. He was implying, of course, ever so gently, the possibility of a suit for breach of contract if Nixon stonewalled. As evidence of Frost's serious-ness, the Anderson column referred to three "crack investiga-tors" whom Frost had at work in Washington. It was a label I found amusing, for I had never quite thought of myself as a crack investigator. Bob Zelnick began referring to us around the office as Cracks 1, 2, and 3. The result was, however, that some important sources appeared out of no-where, and new discoveries (as well as a few useless ones) came our way.

The most sensational windfall consisted of two documents from the Special Prosecutor's Investigation, so sensational that they later were to provide the margin of victory in the quest to capture Proteus. Taken together, the two documents amounted to the government's plan for the interrogation of Richard Nixon, should he ever take the stand as a criminal defendant in federal court. One document was titled "RMN and the Money," and concentrated on the March 21 conversation with John Dean and the desperate search in the weeks that followed to explain away the payment of Howard Hunt's blackmail demand on that day. The memorandum was divided into five parts: RMN statements on the money; his knowledge of hush-money payments before March 21, 1973; the nature of the payment itself; the cover-up of RMN's role in the payment; and RMN's role in developing a "line" to defend against obstruction-of-justice charges. With detailed and extensive references to tape transcripts, many of which were still secret, the overwhelming case was laid out, and Nixon's defense against the case anticipated and refuted. In one of the new tapes, on April 20, 1973, as Nixon was expressing his concern to Haldeman about the March 21 conversation and fearing what Dean was then telling the prosecutors, Nixon's recollection of the talk was that he had said, "Christ, turn over any cash we got." But it was more the thrust and the concept of the overall interrogation document than the individual new quotations that were so valuable. The March 21–April 30 period was mind-numbing in its complexity. The danger was great that Frost could get mired in detail.

I had grave doubts that we could make the period comprehensible to a vast audience on television. But the second document could make it so. There, in cold print, were unsanitized excerpts from the June 20, 1972, Colson conversation I so passionately coveted. The document began with the President's schedule on his first working day back at the White House after the break-in. It listed the meeting with H. R. Haldeman, which later was found to be erased, and then the meeting with Charles Colson from 2:20 to 3:30 p.m. The five references from this Colson conversation were these:

1. Referring tacitly to the break-in, the president said, "If we didn't know better, we would have thought it was deliberately botched." Already he knew some details.

2. Colson said to Nixon, "Bob is pulling it all together. Thus far, I think we've done the right things to date." Right things, Mr. President. How did you take that comment?

3. Referring to the Watergate suspects, Nixon said, "Basically, they are all pretty hard-line guys." Colson interrupted, "You mean Hunt?" And Nixon replied, "Of course, we are just going to leave this where it is, with the Cubans. . . . At times, uh, I just stonewall it."

4. Later, near the end of the conversation, Nixon said, "You look at this damn thing now, and it's gonna be forgotten after a while."

5. And finally, Nixon prophesied, "Oh sure, you know who the hell is going to keep it alive. We're gonna have a court case and indeed . . . the difficulty we'll have

ahead, we have got to have lawyers smart enough to have our people delay, avoiding depositions, of course. . . ."

Perhaps it did not matter to history, or to the American people three years later, that Frost could now establish for the first time that Nixon became part of the Watergate conspiracy three days earlier than was previously known. But in the context of the facts-and-dates approach that Frost and the redoubtable John Birt had insisted upon, with its emphasis on scoops and hard-news investigative journalism, the acquisition of the June 20 excerpts and the February 13 and 14 Colson conversations was critically important. In this climate where everyone seemed to be brushing Frost off as a lightweight and a pushover, startling new discoveries could establish his credentials as a serious interviewer. For me their significance was deeper. If we could keep our possession of the new material secret until it was sprung on Nixon on camera, we might be able to break him out of his studied defenses on Watergate, knock him off balance, and make him wonder about how much new material we had. If he became gun-shy over being confronted with new and damaging revelations, we might get closer to the truth than ever before, perhaps even break Nixon into a confession of guilt. But would our few precious acquisitions hold secret for six months?

For me the task now was to lay the new material into an interrogation strategy, so that the Colson tapes would have their maximum effect. Out of instinct and philosophy, I had already set upon the stance of the hostile interrogation, as opposed to the "objective" information-seeker approach. The House Judiciary Committee had charged Nixon with obstruction of justice on the basis of clear and convincing evidence. He had resigned before he could be impeached by the House and tried by the Senate, but his acceptance of the Ford pardon was considered by the country (and by Gerald Ford himself) as an admission of guilt. Therefore, the appropriate stance for David Frost was to assume Nixon's guilt on all charges and to allow him to try to argue his innocence on some or all counts if he so chose, or to admit guilt on some or all. Later this approach became known within our group as the "adverse inference" we would place upon Nixon's case, a term taken from the minority report of the Judiciary Committee. We would place an adverse inference on any protestation of innocence by Richard Nixon and attack his case with the record.

But how could this best be done so that the approach was subtle and successful and entertaining? What would be the most effective way to fold the discoveries into an interrogation plan so that the surprise, if in the end it was that, would produce the best results? I was no lawyer, much less a prosecutor, so I knew none of the tricks of that trade. For some weeks, however, I had been developing a friendly working relationship with two former prosecutors in the Special Prosecutor's Office, Richard Ben-Veniste and George Frampton. Ben-Veniste had been in charge of the Watergate Task Force under Special Prosecutor Leon Jaworski and had been the chief prosecutor in the cover-up trial. He was a bantam streetfighter, bold and cocky, well aware of his accomplishments, something of a legal swashbuckler in his three-piece suits. His cynical humor about the underside of Washington lawyering often went over my head. Frampton was a Harvard Law graduate whose skeptical eye was somewhat softer than Ben-Veniste's, so that it was a bit easier to see the idealism that lay beneath. Frampton had had the key task of tracking Richard Nixon's involvement in Watergate and had written the so-called "roadmap" memorandum, tracing Nixon's notorious journey through the netherworld of the conspiracy. I had always thought the "roadmap" was simply the statement of facts and events (without conclusions) that the House Judiciary Committee had used as its chief source of evidence. Now I suspected that the two documents in my possession made up the real roadmap. With my new information in hand, I was ready to confront the two young Turks (smart, tough "hot rods," Nixon would call them later, "who hate me with a passion, mostly because of the war").

In my earlier meetings, at the best Washington restaurants—they, too, were eager to take advantage of David Frost's reputation for going first class—I had sensed the profound disappointment of these youthful lawyers at not ever getting Richard Nixon on the witness stand. Their impulse to help me was transparently vicarious. The Frost interrogation of Nixon was likely to be the only grilling Nixon would ever have. They wanted it to succeed. I, in turn, was eager to encourage the feeling in them that Frost and Company would be competent and tough surrogate prosecutors in their place. Armed with their strongest and most secret ammunition against Nixon, I was asking their advice about how it could be used to best advantage. It was not in their interest that it be misused.

When I showed the February 13 and 14 Colson conversations to Frampton and Ben-Veniste, they exchanged glances, and then broke into laughter.

"You've got something no one else has," Frampton said. "Those transcripts must have been placed in the official exhibits by a clerical error." Quietly but with evident relish, they explained the significance of the Colson conversations. They placed Nixon in the conspiracy six weeks earlier than he had publicly admitted. Frampton marked the significant passages for me and then, nearly salivating, showed me how they would have been used with Nixon in the dock. With the memorandum marked "RMN and the Money" (was it his memorandum?—he would never say), we went over the individual points. When we started to get bogged down in detail, my impression was confirmed that this was dangerous material for a television trial. Ben-Veniste, meanwhile, instructed me on the cross-examination of a hostile witness. Frost should allow Nixon to restate his previously held official position about when he learned certain things, and then he should work Nixon backwards in time with the new disclosures. This was another form of what my Chapel Hill academics had urged about eliciting Nixonian generalities and then attacking them with Frostian specifics. Ben-Veniste gave me pointers on the construction of the hostile question. With a tone of disbelief, a good prosecutor was not only eliciting information but also stating his own conclusion.

Thus, a good prosecutor's question was, "Is it still your position, Mr. Nixon, that between 21 March and 30 April 1973 you acted to stop the cover-up and prosecute the guilty?" Answer: yes.

"But in fact, as late as 16 April 1973, you were working out 'scenarios' with Ehrlichman and Haldeman to make John Dean the Watergate scapegoat, weren't you?" Point to Frost.

"By what right were you offering campaign money for the defense of your associates who were charged in a criminal conspiracy?

"Isn't it really true that you never made any effort before 21 March to learn the details of a criminal activity that you knew was going on all around you?"

.   .   .

By late November 1976 I had completed a ninety-six-page, single-spaced interrogation guide for Frost. In each of the six areas of Nixon's criminal involvement, I defined the official Nixonian defense to date, possible lines of questioning, expected responses, and follow-up questions. The practicalities of a television show now began to assert themselves. What could Frost do in a mere ninety minutes? In a minute's television time, only about 125 words could be exchanged. In fact, the show would run only seventy-eight minutes, with twelve minutes earmarked for advertising. Thus I proposed a scheme in which the first half of the show would be devoted to a withering examination of Nixon's criminal culpability; the next twenty minutes to Nixon's court fight to prevent the release of the tapes after Alexander Butterfield's disclosure of them, and to the Saturday Night Massacre. This last landmark event of the Watergate scandal happened on October 20, 1973, when Nixon fired independent Watergate special pros-ecutor Archibald Cox, Attorney General Elliot Richardson, and Deputy Attorney General William Ruckelshaus for not bending to his will. It was the furor over these firings that elicited Nixon's famous statement a month later:

"In all my years of public life, I have never obstructed jus-tice. . . . I've welcomed this kind of examination, because people have got to know whether or not their President is a crook. Well, I'm not a crook!" The last twenty minutes, I proposed, should be devoted to the Final Days and other human material.

In the document, I wrote, "In the first half, David will be a withering cross-examiner; in the next quarter, a political buff fascinated by political strategy; and in the final portion, a sympathetic camp follower looking for human insight." With these different textures, this exercise in entertainment, as I saw it, would have the electric tension of a thriller and the human qualities of a melodrama.

In the early fall, we learned that the tapings with Nixon would be delayed until March 1977. Nixon's wife, Pat, had had a stroke, and this misfortune had put Nixon's goal for the completion of his memoirs behind schedule. The ex-president desperately wanted the delay. Frost had gone to San Clemente and made the most of his opportunity; in return for the delay, Nixon agreed to allow a fifth program, beyond the original four. Further, the ex-president agreed to go forward with the Watergate show, whereas before he had stoutly insisted that he could not talk about Watergate until all the appeals in the cover-up trial had been exhausted. Frost had expressed concern to Nixon that the interviews be aired in the spring of 1977 rather than in the dog days of the summer, when audiences were so much smaller.

"Well, we got one hell of an audience on August 9, 1974," Nixon parried. It was the funniest thing I would ever hear Nixon say.

David had always kept the details of his negotiations absolutely secret from his Washington investigators, and this secrecy bred suspicions. Suspicion turned to paranoia when Frost sent a contract down to Washington in the fall that would bind Zelnick, Stanford, and me to secrecy not only before the airings of the programs, but afterward as well. In an apparent reference to me as the only novelist in the crowd, the contract barred the adaptation of the interviews in fiction, screenplay, or stage production. What if Frost really did have a secret deal with Nixon for soft questions? Or for staying out of certain controversial areas? Or for concentrating on foreign policy endlessly, etc.? Zelnick, Stanford, and I agreed we could be no part of this constraint. Should Frost and Nixon have a deal, it would be our obligation to expose it. So we refused to sign the contract. Frost had a rebellion on his hands.

In typical style, he breezed in from London and took the three of us to lunch at the Rive Gauche. He was charming and funny as always. It was the time of the Earl Butz affair, and Frost had read about it in Japan, where he had been trying to sell the Nixon interviews. Butz had been Nixon's secretary of agriculture and had remained in the Ford Administration, until in the fall of 1976 he was overheard on Air Force One proclaiming the following remarkable thing: "I'll tell you what the coloreds want. It's three things. First, a tight pussy; second, loose shoes; and third, a warm place to shit." The sanitized Japanese translation of Butz's racial slur amused Frost immensely, and he told it to us with all the gusto of a cabaret impresario. "Blacks wanted only three things in life," the Japanese translation went: "pleasant family relations, comfortable footwear, and adequate toilet facilities."

When things got serious, and our objections to the contract as well as other concerns about how tough Frost was prepared to be were expressed, David, for the one and only time, showed us a portion of the contract, specifically the line regarding no editorial control of any kind for Nixon. Frost was careful not to show the following page, which contained the monetary arrangements.

"If any of you have the slightest doubt that I am up to this task, you *should* withdraw now," he said. The third bottle of Pouilly Fuisse came, then the fine cigars. Soon enough we were all very mellow indeed. None of us did withdraw, and work proceeded.

With the Watergate script completed and a month remaining before I needed to return to the university, I concentrated on the human side of Nixon, bearing in mind David Barber's goal of revealing his anti-democratic and banal personality for what it was—or, in Frost's more pedantic construction, to discover what made Richard Nixon tick. David's attitude was that we should know everything we could about the personal rumors, even the wildest ones, that circulated about Nixon, so that the signals could be recognized along the way if they should appear. There were, of course, the long-distance psychiatric profiles, the television-as-psychiatrist's-couch approach, and these I read part in amusement, part in search for a usable anecdote or theory here and there. The best of these was David Abrahamsen's *Nixon vs. Nixon,* a well-researched work, which went as far as psychobiography can without having the patient in the flesh to examine. I read with editorial alertness, deleting the silly theories that so discredit psychohistory, such as Abrahamsen's interest in Nixon's practice of helping his mother mash potatoes on visits home—which, said the good doctor, proved his subject's Oedipal desire always to be close to and please his mother. Later, when I would talk with Abrahamsen in New York, the most interesting advice he would have was "When you get into the enemies list, ask Nixon who in his life has been his greatest enemy. You should have in mind that the answer is Nixon himself."

I talked as well with Dr. Arnold Hutschnecker, the internist/psychiatrist who had treated Nixon in the fifties and early sixties (for impotence, rumor had it), and with Fawn Brodie, Jefferson's and Thaddeus Stevens's biographer, who had begun a psychobiography of Nixon. Brodie would become particularly helpful later, during the tapings in California, but at this stage these consultations bore little fruit.

With these psychology buffs, there were two episodes in Nixon's life about which I was intensely curious. The first came from an interview that Walter Cronkite had conducted with Bebe Rebozo in December 1973, the only such interview to which Rebozo had ever acceded. In it, Cronkite had asked Nixon's pal if it was true that Nixon was a great practical joker (as his daughter Julie had said so). Rebozo giggled in agreement, and Cronkite asked for an example. Rebozo answered as follows:

> We had one time—you know these—somebody gave me a couple of these lady's legs—it looks like a real leg—they're skin-colored and all—they're blown up. And so Abplanalp [Nixon's other pal] was going to

come over to visit us, so we decided to play a trick on him, and we borrowed a wig and a wig stand from a neighbor, put it in a bed with the wig hanging over the thing, and the legs sticking out from under the sheet, and I hid while the President was going to show Abplanalp through the house. Bob came in, and when he saw that, he was . . . he . . . he [laughs] didn't . . . he didn't know whether to act like he didn't see it, or leave, or what, but it was quite a riot. But I was hiding around the corner with a flash camera and took a picture of Abplanalp hovering over this figure in bed. But it's . . . it's . . . we just . . . it's hard to recall incidents, because . . . but he . . . but he really has a rare and quick sense of humor, very quick.

That seemed to me to be a psychiatric bonanza, a glimpse into the dark world of his friendship with Rebozo and Abplanalp. Dr. Abrahamsen would interpret this "practical joke" to me as "exceedingly immature sexually, the kind of thing eight- or nine-year-old boys would do." Reporters had noted how often Nixon flew to Key Biscayne, left Pat and the daughters at the "Florida White House," and then helicoptered over to Robert Abplanalp's home on Grand Cay with Bebe Rebozo. Why was this one of his favorite hangouts? Did Pat Nixon complain about being left behind? What did Nixon and Rebozo and Abplanalp have in common that made this a favorite place for relaxation? What was so entertaining, Walter Cronkite asked Rebozo, about the two men sitting together for hours without exchanging a word?

Later, Fawn Brodie drew my attention to a curious exchange of letters in 1971 and 1973 between Rebozo and Richard Danner, the Howard Hughes contact in Las Vegas. The letters appeared as exhibits in the Senate Watergate Investigation into the Hughes/Rebozo connection, and they opened with Danner writing Rebozo about an advertisement for the Royal Biscayne Hotel. "Frankly," wrote Danner, "it aroused many speculations in my mind, basically how could an attractive person, with obvious charms, have been able to come over to Key Biscayne repeatedly and invade the domain of the man-eating tiger (pardon the expression). . . . Those certain psychological changes I detected in you a couple of years ago such as constant invitations for me to stay at your house, have finally changed the direction of your interests. Of course, there is a final thought, namely, that you have fallen behind in your homework. . . ."

Rebozo responded indignantly, "Only a third-degree depraved mind could have given birth to thoughts such as those expressed therein. Maybe, on the other hand, it is the frustration bit you experienced by 'misreading' the invitation to stay at my house, which I have on occasion inadvisedly extended. Frankly, you are not my type."

In 1973, however, after a visit between the two men, Rebozo would write a more affectionate thank-you note to Danner: "It was good getting together with you after so many years. Sorry father time has sort of caught up with me, and I was unable to get through the entire evening. Some day when you reach my age you'll know what I mean. Come on down, even though I can't reciprocate the lavish hospitality, I'll afford you the 'queen for a day' room."

Danner responded, "I hope this finds you in good health and spirits. One of these days I will try to sneak off and come down and spend a quiet visit with you and submit myself to the indignities and penuriousness one associates with you (when you are on your best behavior)."

What one was to do with this material, I hardly knew, but it did seem to confirm the importance of delving into the curious society of these men (if there was any way that Frost could subtly do so). Dr. Abrahamsen suggested this form of question for the Nixon/Rebozo relationship: "Why was this friendship with Bebe Rebozo so deeply rooted?"

The second episode about which I needed advice was Nixon's farewell address to his staff before, on August 9, 1974, he boarded the plane for San Clemente. In that tearful, embarrassingly maudlin exercise in free association, Nixon had remembered his old man on the poorest lemon ranch in California, and his mother, about whom no books would be written, but she was a saint. He quoted from a book about Teddy Roosevelt's young wife, "fair, pure, joyous as a maiden," and then she died, and TR thought "the light had passed from his life," but, he went on, "He was a man." Was this Pat Nixon he was really talking about? The psychiatrists were feasting on this cornucopia of psychic suggestion, and Fawn Brodie called the speech the most important of Nixon's career—to the biographers. I already had David Frost's promise to play the speech for Nixon on the set, with the cameras on his face as he watched.

The Final Days would, of course, be the most fertile ground for examining Nixon's inner recesses and, for that matter, delving into the universal themes of humiliation and defeat. There were also important questions of political process. Had Nixon really told a group of congressmen in the last few days that he could go into the next room and press a button, and twenty million people would be dead? Had Secretary of Defense James Schlesinger really told the Joint Chiefs in the last days that any order from the White House for troop movements or military action had to be countersigned by him? Was this not the removal of the President's war-making powers, and, in effect, a coup d'état?

Furthermore, I had unearthed a document that demonstrated that Nixon was not sobbing with congressmen, Henry Kissinger, or his family all the time in those final days. He was also putting his mind hardheadedly to the vulturous historians and biographers who were bound to descend upon him later. In *Nixon vs. Nixon,* Dr. Abrahamsen had made much of a film titled *Nixon: A Self-Portrait,* made by the Republican Party in the 1968 presidential campaign, when it was thought by party leaders that Nixon was in need of a little humanizing. A sympathetic portrait of Nixon about his family and upbringing, the film was the only document (other than Bela Kornitzer's 1960 biography, *The Real Nixon*) where Nixon talked frankly about himself. When I called the Republican National Committee looking for the film and hoping for a screening, I was informed that "someone from the White House" had come over in the final week of Nixon's presidency and taken away every bit of Nixoniana they held in their library. I was on to something. A week later I found the proof I sought. At the time I was looking into Nixon's taxes. Taxes, like his misuse of government funds at San Clemente and Key Biscayne, were the cutting edge, for they were abuses of power that directly enriched Nixon's personal fortune. Thus they applied to his personal corruption as opposed to his political corruption. With Watergate, taxes were the other area where Nixon had escaped criminal prosecution only because he was president.

But it was a complicated matter, involving the gift of presidential papers to the National Archives and taking an enormous tax deduction of $432,000 on the basis of a backdated deed of gift. Leaving all that aside for the moment, in the course of that research I acquired from the National Archives a letter from Richard Nixon, dated August 8, 1974, his last full working day at the White House. The letter changed the terms of Nixon's gift of papers to the nation. Instead of opening access to them after his incumbency as president (in effect, August 10, 1974), the Nixon letter locked up the papers until 1985. What presence of mind! Here was a president about to resign in disgrace and humiliation, who was cool enough to concern himself with frustrating the work of historians who would want to analyze him.

The document had a further implication. Under the old law in which a public official could take a tax deduction for a gift of papers, the gift had to fulfill a criterion of "present interest" as opposed to "future interest." In specific terms, that meant that while a gift in 1968 with scholarly access in 1974 might loosely be considered of "present interest," a 1968 gift with access seventeen years later would clearly not be. Therefore, changing the terms to 1985 underscored in one more conclusive way the illegitimacy of Nixon's tax deductions.

THE WHITE HOUSE

Washington

AUGUST 8, 1974

Dear Sir:

Pursuant to the provisions of numbered paragraph 1 of the Chattel Deed from Richard M. Nixon to the United States of America, dated December 30, 1968, I hereby modify the provisions of access as follows:

1. The undersigned shall have the right of access to any and all of the Materials and the right to copy or to have copied any and all of the Materials by any means of his selection, and to take and retain possession of any or all such copies for any purpose whatsoever. Prior to January 1, 1985, no person or persons shall have the right of access to such Materials except the undersigned and those who may be designated in writing by the undersigned, and in the case of any person or persons so designated, such right of access

shall be limited to those Materials as shall be described in the instrument by which he, she, it or they shall be designated, and for the purposes specified in such instrument; and, if such instrument shall so provide, the person or persons designated therein shall have the further right to copy such of the Materials as shall be described in such instrument and to take and retain possession of such copies for such purposes as shall be specified in said instrument. The undersigned shall have the right and power at any time during his life-time to modify or remove this restriction as to any or all of the Materials and/or to grant access to any group or groups of persons by notification in writing to the General Services Administration or other appropriate agency of The United States of America.

Sincerely,

Honorable Arthur F. Sampson
Administrator
General Services Administration
Washington, D.C. 20405

As an addendum to my script, I advised Frost to show Nixon the letter, and then ask, "Why, Mr. President, were you deliberately trying to obstruct the work of historians with this action?"

One final task remained before I returned to North Carolina: a talk with John Dean. I'd been trying to catch him on one of his trips to the East Coast, ever since the Republican Party Convention, when he was the reporter for *Rolling Stone*. His natural role now was to promote himself and his new book. Other contacts with Nixon associates (except indirectly for Charles Colson) had not been productive. Ehrlichman had refused to talk. Haldeman wanted money. Ray Price had talked about Watergate as a "bee-sting on the heel of the Nixon Presidency." Fred Buzhardt, Nixon's personal attorney who had revealed the existence of the eighteen-and-a-half-minute gap, thought Nixon got a particularly raw deal on the tax matter. Bruce Herschensohn railed about the double standard in the news media. It was all predictable fare, and with some, particularly Price, Herschensohn, and Colson, the certainty that our interests would be conveyed to San Clemente was evident. So the opposition learned more about us from these talks than we learned from them.

By the time Bob Zelnick and I went to see Dean in New York, our work in Washington was virtually complete. We had little hope that Dean would say anything new or interesting.

Why should he? He was known for husbanding his disclosures, releasing them with care. The week previous he'd made
headlines with a thirdhand story about Nixon admitting to
Colson that the House Un-American Activities Committee
(HUAC) had built a typewriter in the Alger Hiss case. With
two new books out on Hiss, the question of whether Hiss
had been framed by Nixon and Company was again active.

We waited in the lobby of the St. Regis Hotel before going
up to Dean's suite. Zelnick wondered if he was obliged to
shake Dean's hand. His loathing seemed excessive, for Old Zel
had been quite excited about talking with Ehrlichman on the
telephone. "Good luck to you," I could remember Zelnick
signing off on his call to Ehrlichman. "Wisdom," as Ehrlichman was known in the White House, was about to go into jail
in New Mexico, but the film adaptation of his novel *Washington Behind Closed Doors* was then in production. He didn't seem
to need any luck.

Dean greeted us at the door cordially. He was deeply
tanned and beautifully tailored. He had the look of a showbiz
personality now, and we would constantly be interrupted by
calls from his publicity agent. Dean was a commodity these
days, lecturing at a half million per year, his open chronicle
of moral and political degradation on the best-seller list
for many weeks, thirty hours of discussions with David
Susskind's writer for the television dramatization of *Blind
Ambition*. Mrs. Dean, meanwhile, she of the enormous ear-
rings, was mimicking Nixon on *The Mike Douglas Show*.

Dean sells. Dean moves. Dean knew it.

"What would you ask Nixon now?" I inquired.

Recently he had said on the lecture circuit that one day he would like to talk again with Nixon. Why? To apologize? To explain his own personal weaknesses? To be forthright finally about his motives?

"I would like to be in your shoes," he replied in his flat monotone. Our shoes? Dean in our shoes? So ghoulish was his notion that I did not grasp its import at first.

"Yes," he repeated. "I would like to be his interrogator," and he proceeded with his fantasy about how he would go about it.

It was time for me to escape from this nightmare for a while.

PART II

Hollywood

HOLLYWOOD! THE BEVERLY HILTON! Offices in Century City, across from 20th Century Fox! It would be hard to go back to the farm after this. Nixon was show business, and it was showtime.

When I arrived at the Beverly Hilton on March 16 and called David, the hotel operator conveyed the message that he welcomed me to Los Angeles, and we'd get together in a few hours, but at present he was engaged. I assumed his engagement was with one of his many business associates, since that was the rule. With another call, however, I learned he was huddling with H. R. Haldeman. This news both intrigued and pleased me. In the four visits that David had made to Washington in the six months that his crack investigators were at work, he had expressed his intention to talk personally to a number of key figures. Zelnick and I had made a list for him, stressing that in several instances, where important figures would not see us, they might see Frost. Among these were Alexander Haig, who would be the best source on the last-minute negotiations on the Nixon pardon, and James Schlesinger, who might talk about any extraordinary precautions taken in the Defense Department in the Final Days. (Schlesinger, his former press aide William Beecher told me, had the stuffed-shirt propensity for seeing only the real luminary in a project like ours. "He has a highly tuned sense of protocol," Beecher had said.) But David never did make the time for his own personal interviewing. By the time he arrived in Los Angeles, a week before the interviews were to begin, the only significant people he had talked with were Richard Helms (whom he had seen in Iran while filming a documentary financed by the Shah) and Anthony Ulasewicz. With Ulasewicz, Watergate bagman turned slapstick comic, David seemed to be developing a kind of cabaret camaraderie, whereby they would trade one-liners with each other.

So it was good that he was talking with Haldeman, but what deal had David made with him? In response to my letter requesting an interview in the fall, Haldeman had said on the phone that the Frost interviews were obviously a commercial enterprise, and how much was David willing to pay for consultation? The reply from Marv Minoff, Frost's business manager, was that we would pay scale, about $350, as if it were an appearance on *The Tonight Show.* That was the end of the fall overture.

When the Frost team—Frost, Zelnick, producer Birt, manager Minoff, and I—met that night for the first time on the West Coast, David reported that he had had a fascinating three-hour lunch with Haldeman, and that naturally the question of a fee arose. David had offered $5,000 for Haldeman to sit down with us for six hours. Haldeman had appeared unimpressed. (For one used to having $350,000 in cash in his safe, or to being paid $100,000 for a *60 Minutes* interview, who could blame him?) He promised to have his lawyer get in touch with Minoff the following day. Both Zelnick and I opposed the offer. We had only a week to plan and to brief David before the first taping session. Quite

obviously, Frost had not focused on the content of his interviews even at this late date. We would have to put everything
else aside to plan for a secondary, private interrogation of
Haldeman. David salivated at the notion of Haldeman novel-
ties and argued that we wouldn't have to plan ahead for the
Haldeman talks. But Bob Zelnick, the lawyer here, replied
that he could not talk with Haldeman without considerable
planning.

The subject was batted around for several hours. For the
first time ever, as the innocent in the enterprise, I felt myself
being drawn into Watergate-like negotiations. This was
Howard Hunt writ small. We were trying to recruit a thug
with a little cash, but what assurance did we have that he
would tell us anything useful? None, David admitted wistfully. Why wouldn't he do the same thing with us that he had
done with several newspaper articles he had written: ask
unproductive, rhetorical questions like "Was Alexander Butterfield a CIA agent? I don't know." No reason why not,
David replied. But he still wouldn't mind the experience. He
had that Woodward-and-Bernstein gleam in his eye again.

So it was left that if Haldeman accepted David's offer of
$5,000, we would consider how to proceed, balancing a
Haldeman talk against other exigencies. The following day,
Haldeman's lawyer called Minoff with a counteroffer: $25,000
for the first two hours of consultation, with Reston and
Zelnick; $15,000 for the second two hours; $10,000 for the
final two, a total of $50,000. So what did I expect? The matter

became a house joke for the next week, David patting Bob and me on the back for the $5,000 we had saved him.

It had been my hope since the start of my involvement in the project that the first hours of interviewing with Nixon would be spent on human material. The notion seemed obvious: early on, Frost should establish the dimensions of this personality with sympathetic, personal questions. Exhibit concern for Pat Nixon after her stroke, and for Nixon himself after his phlebitis—that sort of thing. What kind of life he had established in San Clemente in retirement (eschewing, of course, the word *exile*). David himself was fresh from an interview with Harold Wilson, who had just resigned as the British prime minister. In the beginning of the interview, he had used a cricket analogy to describe the feeling-out stage at the start of an electronic memoir. "I'll just ask you a few general questions at first, so that you, as the batter, can get your eye," Frost had opened.

"And the bowler can find his range," Wilson parried.

As the radical on the team, I had joked that the first question ought to be, "Why did you lie when you told that Florida audience, 'I am not a crook'?"

"And then we can play soft music for the remaining twenty-four hours," had been David's riposte. Technically, under the terms of his contract, Nixon simply had to sit with Frost for twenty-four hours, although, as David had told Jack Anderson, silence would hardly have been in the spirit of the contract.

David was optimistic. Nixon's staff had told him that Nixon was now ready "to confront his past." To Mike Wallace, David had said, "I'm hoping for a cascade of candor."

"A cascade of candor? From Richard Nixon?" Wallace replied, incredulous. The skeptical note in his voice expressed the national consensus.

Soon after I arrived in Los Angeles, I had dinner with Fawn Brodie. By that time she had read more than two hundred books relating in one way or another to Richard Nixon. She was about ready to begin writing about Nixon's childhood. Her psychobiography, she estimated, would take her four years, and unlike her other biographies, of Jefferson, Thaddeus Stevens, and Joseph Smith, there were many living figures to interview as well. She had already experienced the low points (which I shared) of dealing with such depressing material, but she pressed on because "the villain is fascinating." The villain, she was sure, would never see her, so once again Frost was the surrogate biographer, on top of his role as surrogate prosecutor.

I was eager to engage Fawn Brodie's imagination and wisdom in my cause of stalking the personal Nixon. Already it was becoming clear that Birt, the foreigner who had no feel for American emotions, and Zelnick, the Washington-trained journalist, were squeezing out any time for a psychological line of questioning. A curious concept of the "substantive question," as opposed to the soft question, had appeared, and personal material was fast becoming soft. Birt introduced the notion of the "self-serving" answer. This whole project is self-serving for Nixon, I responded, and his answers would be most self-serving of all when he was allowed to act "presidential," appearing to be the reasonable leader considering reasonable options, in a facts-and-dates examination. This was especially true when those facts and dates were rapidly slipping from the mind of the American people. A response that went to character and political or moral depravity would be fertile and would be noticed as something new, I said. This disagreement never abated within the Frost camp during the full six weeks of taping and editing.

In the day before the first session, David set us all an interesting task: to devise several "litmus questions" so we could determine instantly by the color of his answer what Nixon's stance toward us would be. My instinct was that in the beginning there should be some large philosophical strokes that not only determined Nixon's posture of either bitterness or remorse, but also accentuated the historical nature of the discussion. It would be well, I thought, to begin on a high, dignified plain, before moving into the trenches.

1. On exile:

These lines are from Shakespeare, and are spoken by King Richard II, the abdicated king: "Oh, that I were as great as is my grief, or lesser than my name. Or that I could forget what I have been, or not remember what I must be now."

Do these lines from Shakespeare have any bearing on your feeling since your resignation?

2. On lying:

In your acceptance speech in 1968 in Miami Beach, you told the assemblage: "Let us begin by committing ourselves to truth. To see it like it is and tell it like it is, to find the truth, to speak the truth, to live the truth. The time has come for honest government in America." When you left the presidency, you were being called a "virtuoso in deception." Even your longtime supporter Barry Goldwater said at the end that you had told "one lie too many."

How did this happen?

3. On remorse:

You told Rabbi Baruch Korff in a taped interview, May 13, 1974: "The most important factor is that the individual must know, deep inside, that he is right. He must believe that. If, for example, these charges on Watergate and the cover-up were true, nobody would have to ask me to resign. I wouldn't serve for one minute if they were true. But I know they are not true, and therefore I will stay here." You told Rabbi Korff this eight days after you had listened to the June 23, 1972, tape, the so-called smoking gun.

Were you to relive this interview with Rabbi Korff, would you change what you told him?

4. On stress:

Perhaps no other American political figure has faced the kind of pressure you endured, over such a long period of time.

In your political career, you have consulted with several psychiatrists from time to time, but in the hour of your greatest turmoil, you relied on political cronies.

Why didn't you seek professional help in the period of your greatest need?

5. On living with himself:

You also spoke to Rabbi Korff about a Quaker concept of Peace at the Center:

"My peace at the center," you said, "means that whatever the storms are that may be roaring up or down, that the individual must have and retain that peace within him, and that will see him through all the adversity."

Your storms no longer rage around you now, but as you have pondered your mistakes and misjudgments, have you been able to retain your peace at the center?

6. On depression after defeat:

In your book *Six Crises,* you developed an ideology of crisis, and you discovered what you called a "fundamental rule of conduct in crisis":

"The point of greatest danger . . . occurs after the crisis of battle is over, regardless of whether it has resulted in victory or defeat. The individual is spent physically, emotionally, and mentally lets down."

Your crises are over now; have you been able to guard against depression or against bitterness toward those who disserved you?

Bob Zelnick was the Frost contact with the White House in exile, and he had been to San Clemente several times before I arrived on the West Coast. Old Zel's counterpart was one Ken Khachigian, an unprepossessing Iranian who peered suspiciously out through thick glasses, who smoked thin cigars and wore Mickey Mouse ties. In the Nixon literature, Khachigian appears only once, to my knowledge, in Jonathan Schell's *Illusion of Power,* where, along with Patrick Buchanan, he is given credit for arranging phony telegrams to be sent to *Time* and *Newsweek* supporting Nixon after the Cambodian invasion. Jeb Stuart Magruder had referred to this as "our letter-writing system." I wanted as little to do with Khachigian as possible.

The other name I had heard frequently mentioned was Jack Brennan, *Colonel* Brennan, Nixon's chief of staff. The mere term "chief of staff" had a curiously nostalgic ring, given Brennan's predecessors, and I would have thought that for public-relations reasons alone the term would have been retired. Of course, in exile, Nixon had no public relations. What rank did Napoleon's aides have on St. Helena, I wondered.

To my disappointment, the tapings would take place not at Casa Pacifica, but ten miles north, in a wealthy development complete with security gate, called Monarch Bay. The Coast Guard station near the Nixon offices in San Clemente contained a LORAN facility, which guided shipping traffic along the West Coast. The radar signals the station emitted were damaging to television videotape. In the days of the Imperial

Presidency, the LORAN station was shut down when Nixon gave a television speech from San Clemente, but the Coast Guard refused to do that for Frost.

The wicked LORAN signal was discovered by the director for the Nixon interviews, Jörn Winther. Winther was a delightful Dane, whom Frost always called "Danish Pastry." (Winther in turn called Frost "English Muffin.") The director had gone to San Clemente several months earlier to make the technical arrangements and have his audience with Nixon. He remembered vividly joking with Nixon about how he might brighten up the Exile's bland office for the tapings by hanging a Danish flag on the wall. Nixon, the good ole boy, had laughed, and then had walked over to a three-foot globe of the world, had spun it vigorously, and, when it stopped, had placed his finger on Denmark as if, as the geography teacher, he felt Winther might need a refresher. His lesson did not end there.

"This is China," Nixon continued. "There are 700 million people living there, as opposed to 100 million in the Middle East." He spun the globe to the Middle East. "And 250 million in Russia. Where do you suppose most of the troubles in our world have come from?"

Jörn felt as if he should raise his hand.

"Not Denmark," he quipped. Winther and the other technicians present would never forget that scene. The memory of Nixon hovering over his globe and spinning it with both hands was somehow deeply frightening. It was vaguely reminiscent of a scene in Charlie Chaplin's *The Great Dictator*.

At 7:30 a.m. on March 23, 1977, we gathered in the lobby of the Beverly Hilton and piled into David's gray Mercedes for the eighty-mile trip to Monarch Bay. The hour-and-a-half trip was to become a key briefing time for David, especially when he was ill-prepared for the day's session. Only later would I develop the equanimity to feel that the die was basically cast before I arrived in California. If David Frost had not taken the time in advance to build a conceptual base for the murky areas of foreign policy and domestic turmoil, he could not take it on board in the final moments before he went on camera. John Birt, who had worked with Frost on other interviews of political figures, like Ali Bhutto of Pakistan, tried to calm our discreetly phrased fears about Frost's lack of preparation. As a "performer" who had done this many times before, David knew how much preparation he had to do for a successful interview, Birt protested. Frost never overprepared. Like Superman, Frost might appear Clark Kentish for a distressingly long time, and then suddenly, unexpectedly, just as the villain was about to take over Metropolis, off would come the shirt, and pow! the knock-out punch. Unpersuaded, I screwed up my face quizzically.

Sixty miles down the San Diego Freeway, we exited on the Crown Valley Parkway, proceeded along the Avenida de la Presidente, past brassy new condominiums in the lush hills with flags flying, to Monarch Bay. A distinctly imperial flavor marked the last leg of the trip. Where were Nixon's heralds to announce us as we passed?

The house rented for the tapings for $6,000 belonged to an industrialist, Harold Smith, a gun fancier and gunsmith. When Marv Minoff, our businessman, had arrived to look the house over weeks before, Mr. Smith came to the door with a .38 revolver strapped to his hip and proudly showed Minoff a cupboard full of some fifty shotguns and rifles in his den. When Nixon came, the Secret Service always carefully guarded the Smith arsenal. In the sprawling split-level, the master bedroom was reserved for Nixon. Next to it, a smaller bedroom was our headquarters. Down eight steps, on the ground level, in the den, the Nixon staff—Brennan, Khachigian, and Diane Sawyer—hung out. In both our room and the Nixon staff room below, monitors had been installed. The set itself had been designed by Los Angeles interior decorators, and David had been pleased with the comfortable yellow chairs and yellow curtains behind his chair. The background behind Nixon was a bookcase full of volumes of presidential papers from the Nixon, Johnson, and Kennedy presidencies. On this first day of taping, a blue vase placed amid the presidential volumes was found to meld into the distinctly blue cast of Nixon's hair under the lights, and it was removed. On the table behind Frost, fittingly, there was a white porcelain statuette of two figures, dancing.

I was closeted with David and Old Zel when Nixon arrived that first day. We were going over last-minute details of substance while David had his hair washed, blow-dried, and set by Ken Wensovic, the makeup man whose credits included *Maude* and *A Salute to the Beatles*. Unexpectedly, Nixon appeared in our doorway. He was a larger man than I expected, well over six feet, with an erect, rather proud carriage. He looked fit and healthy, well tanned with an orangey hue, and dressed in politician's blue serge. David greeted him effusively and flatteringly, as he would do every taping day, careful to call him "Mr. President," which seemed to be the unspoken imperative for all. Surrounded by a covey of producers, staffers, and Secret Service men, the performers moved to the set. I followed this parade at a distance, curious, transfixed, overwhelmed by the spectacle. All the hard work was coming to fruition. The troubles with Birt and Zelnick, the depression over the soul-shriveling material, the anxieties over David's performance receded in my mind. I was here, part of this important event, whatever its outcome might be. Despite my skepticism that this extravaganza would ever take place, we were about to begin.

The principals took their seats. The seconds repaired to their places. The director said, "Three minutes." The makeup man straightened lapels and dabbed foreheads with powder one last time. Nixon placed his handkerchief on the table beside him. (Frost had promised that Nixon could pat his sweat away when his interviewer asked a question, and this patting would not be on camera in the final cut.) The seconds ticked away. Nixon was talking about the 100,000 letters his wife had received, mostly from schoolchildren, after her stroke. Frost made a joke about the camera crew speaking only Turkish, so being unable to leak the contents of the talks. Nixon seemed not to hear. He did not laugh, or take notice. This was the big comeback bout. He was more concerned with whether his collar was riding up on his shirt.

·   ·   ·

The contract between Frost and Nixon called for twenty-four hours of taping, which would be boiled down into four ninety-minute television programs, loosely defined as foreign policy, domestic affairs, Watergate, and a catchall, "Nixon the Man." That left six hours for each area, if the tapings were handled with discipline. But there were good arguments for Frost, the experienced performer, not to be too rigid about these formulations. From the beginning, Nixon and his people wanted a definition of Watergate. Their view on the matter was, as it were, perfectly clear. Watergate was an umbrella for everything negative: not just the cover-up, but the abuses of power in the IRS, CIA, and FBI, the personal tax issue, Ellsberg, the dispute over illegal expenditures on presidential houses, the sale of ambassadorships, the enemies list, and the Huston Plan. Try fitting all that into six hours of discussion. It was a transparent effort to dilute and shorten our concentration on the issue that had driven Nixon from office.

To us, of course, Watergate had a narrow meaning: the Watergate break-in and cover-up. Other abuses fell into domestic affairs or Nixon the Man. Tax cheating, for example, had to do with Nixon the Corrupt Man, not Watergate. The Washington research and planning for the entire program, separate from my Watergate script, had been called "all non-Watergate sleazy Nixon" for short.

In California, I soon became accustomed to talking as much about strategy as about substance with Frost. Frost and Birt argued that we should resist tendering our narrow Watergate definition for fear that Nixon would time the Watergate minutes to the second, and simply announce at some point, midsentence, that the six hours for Watergate had expired. It was an argument I never completely comprehended. My interest was to protect a pristine six full hours for my "area," and I felt the Nixonians would be timing anyway. But I readily admitted my naïveté at these subtle business negotiations, expressed my view, and let it ride. On this level, Frost, Birt, and Bob Zelnick, with his legal training, knew what they were doing, I concluded. Frost, after all, was one of the great entrepreneurs in the world. So, at least, I had been told.

My concern that we were being maneuvered came later.

The plan for the first taping day was that David would move right into foreign policy after he asked the litmus question and talked a bit about the resignation and departure. But it did not turn out that way, much to my delight. Instead, using gymnastics rather than a cricket analogy, the session was a free-form exercise of bitterness and schmaltz. Nixon blamed

Haldeman for not destroying the tapes. He described weeping at Eisenhower's death and with Kissinger over his own resignation. ("That you should have to leave office is a crime," he quoted Kissinger as saying.) He described Tip O'Neill as "shrewd and ruthless," and John Doar, the counsel to the House Impeachment Committee, as a "brilliant prosecutor." He complained about his defense counsel in the impeachment hearings, Albert Jenner, who, he said, had deserted the cause and left his case to be made by "a very young lawyer," Sam Garrison. His language on the tapes was no worse than Ike's barracks-room talk, and Harry Truman, getting better marks today than then, pardoned fifteen men in Kansas City's Pendergast machine for vote-stealing. In Nixon's pantheon of virtues, being a "controlled person" was equated with being a strong person. He, Pat Nixon, and Ray Price were all strong, because they were controlled. On Wednesday, August 7, 1974, Tricia had come into his office, thrown her arms around him, "kissed me and cried. She so seldom cries. And I said, 'Don't cry, honey.' She said, 'Daddy, I know I shouldn't, but you know, except for Eddie [her husband], I just want you to know you're the finest man I know.' " And Julie? The same day she had left a note tacked on his pillow. "Dear Daddy, whatever you do, I will support you, but wait a week or ten days. Just go through the fire a little longer. I love you. Julie." Imagine a daughter asking her father to go through the fire a little longer. But fair was fair: he had made her go through the fire for over a year, protesting his innocence. Perhaps this was Julie's revenge.

On the set monitor, Frost rolled the tape of Nixon's Farewell Address, and allowed that he had probably seen it a number of times in the past two years. Oh no, Nixon responded, he had never listened to the audio of a speech, or watched himself on television, or ever practiced a performance like Winston Churchill before a mirror. The categorical statement reminded me of biographer Fawn Brodie's category of "Unnecessary Nixon Lies."

"It is true I have a tendency to look down when I'm thinking, and with my heavy eyebrows—I had them trimmed this morning—because they [who were they?] tell me you should keep them trimmed and then the audience can see your eyes. Or [they tell me] you shouldn't gesture so much because your hands get in front of your face. Well, maybe that's good. Maybe the hands are better looking than the face."

Here was the vanity and insecurity, the preoccupation with appearance within a denial of it. Here was the fascination with television technique that political scientist James David Barber had urged me to go after.

"My advice to a budding politician who wants to be a success on television," he continued, "is to be yourself. Get all the recommendations of the experts, but be as natural as you can. If you start looking at television tapes of your speeches, you're going to become self-conscious."

Then, cleverly, Nixon tried to undermine Frost's credentials early as a serious journalist. "In your profession, when you were at the Blue Angel, or on *That Was the Week That Was,* you had to feel you were an actor. You must have looked at the tapes and said, 'Now, how could I do this better?' "

Even more cleverly and deftly, Frost displayed the Nixon half-gainer within a double flip. Frost asked, if Nixon were a historian and were granted a paragraph—a paragraph—to describe the Nixon presidency, how would he do it? Frost's granting him only a paragraph had a quixotic quality. Nixon went on for minutes about building a structure of peace, with more progress toward the goal in his five and one-half years than any other period since World War II, about ending the Vietnam War "in an honorable way," in a way that deterred aggression abroad, about the China initiative.

"Those are some of the positive things you hope history will say about the Nixon Administration," Frost interjected. "What negative things do you think it will say about the Administration?"

"The primary negative will be that the Nixon Administration engaged in political activities which led to the resignation. In other words, the bugging of the Democratic headquarters and so forth. Here we have, of course, a double standard. . . ." Oh, and one other point where he should get credit besides Vietnam, China, Arms Control, and the Middle East was his strong presidential leadership in pushing the desegregation of Southern schools. He went on with that for several minutes.

How had it happened? This miraculous genuflection to the negative side in one sentence, and the continuation of his litany of achievements. No remorse, no apology. We would have to extract one.

Frost tried to recoup. "You're saying that in your judgment history will pay more attention to your achievements in foreign policy than it will to Watergate or to abuses of power?"

"What history says about this Administration will depend on who writes the history. . . . Winston Churchill once told a critic that history would treat him well. 'How do you know?' the critic asked. 'Because I intend to write it,' Churchill replied."

I can't wait for the *Memoirs,* I thought.

. . .

On the ride back to Beverly Hills, David and I were ebullient. Birt and Zelnick were depressed. We had acquired thirty or forty minutes of usable footage, I felt: crying with Kissinger, the reasons for not destroying the tapes, the bitterness and the blaming, the absence of voluntary grief or remorse. The spectacle of forcing Nixon to watch his farewell speech was a kind of punishment that would provide a psychic release for an American audience. Psychic release at the outset was vital, I thought. He had said that he had decided finally to resign on July 23, 1974, when he called Governor George Wallace in the hope that Wallace would pressure Alabama congressman Walter Flowers to vote against impeachment, and Wallace refused to help. (Nixon did not mention that the following day the Supreme Court ruled against him on the tapes.)

True, some good Frost questions had elicited some banal, unusable Nixon answers. The best example had come in a discussion of Nixon's Farewell Address.

"At the end of your speech, you said, 'Always remember, others may hate you, but those who hate you don't win unless you hate them, and then you destroy yourself.' When you said that, was it a lesson for other people, or a lesson that you ought to have observed yourself ?"

The Nixon answer bogged us down with an anecdote of Chief Newman, his Indian football coach at Whittier College, who had taught young Richard that he didn't go for that stuff about being a good loser. "Show me a good loser, and I'll show you a loser," the Chief had counseled. "When you lose, you ought to get mad, but get mad at yourself, not the other guy. Get mad at yourself, or what you did." So we were learning that Nixon could not rise to the grand themes of hate and humiliation that his life exemplified. I was relieved that Shakespeare on grief had not been quoted to him, for I did not relish the thought of Richard II and Bolingbroke being greeted with Chief Newman and the Pendergast gang.

Birt and Zelnick felt the session had been soft and self-serving. The taped answer had been allowed to drone on for twenty-three minutes without interruption. There had been no plan or thrust to the questioning. The pudding had no theme. Nixon's anecdotes became Nixon's filibusters, and they often bore no relevance to the questions. Frost must devise methods to cut the ex-president off when he began a maudlin anecdote. He must be more disciplined, must shoot for sustained and relevant debate. The solution was to keep the subject close to the nub of fact, leaving him no room for diversion or maneuver.

The following morning, as became the custom, we all watched the tape of the previous session. For this review, the syndicated columnist Joseph Kraft, who was in Los Angeles, joined us, and his comments were incisive. He urged Frost to study the Nixon cadence. When the President's voice trailed off, as if at the end of a paragraph, David should jump in with a question. The problem was delicate and difficult, all agreed, but Frost's body language was far too relaxed. David could not allow himself to swap generalizations with Nixon. He must think in terms of one-paragraph answers; the subject could be allowed no second paragraphs. Nixon's filibusters must be made to look ludicrous, and Frost's interruptions made to look justified. Closely linked questions must become the rule. When Nixon started off on a tangent, Frost must be prepared to say, as John Birt put it, "Hang on. We're getting off the point here," or "I'm sorry, I still don't understand, but we really must move on."

Tone was crucial. Firmness and control without disrespect must be the rule. The show must appear to feed on its own disclosures. "The process by which the interview is conducted must look as interesting as the information gleaned," Kraft advised.

In the coming four sessions on foreign policy, the nub-of-fact strategy was adopted. To this way of thinking, I had made a partial conversion in the months before. With Watergate I was persuaded that a factual interrogation, rather than my early notion of a thematic approach, would work better, not only because history possessed such a void of fact when it came to Nixon's diplomatic actions, but because the vast viewing audience was more aware of the factual record of Watergate than any other issue. But with foreign policy and domestic affairs, I was afraid that the audience was neither knowledgeable nor interested, save the minute community of diplomatic historians and the political scientists. Nonetheless, since those areas were not my responsibility but Bob Zelnick's, I stayed mum. I was certainly no foreign-policy expert, and I viewed the foreign-policy show as Nixon's quid pro quo for my Watergate interrogation.

In his foreign-policy script, Bob Zelnick had defined eight topics for examination: Vietnam and Cambodia, Chile and the CIA, Salt II, the Kissinger relationship, Soviet-American relations, the Middle East, the Indo-Pakistan conflict, and China. During the coming sessions on these topics, I played the role of the intelligent nonexpert, commenting in post-taping sessions on Nixon statements I found striking. I doubt that my comments were of much use. I was too much a product of my own generation, especially its horror over

Vietnam, to be interested in the mechanics of diplomacy, especially when the "diplomacy" resulted in the carpet-bombing of Hanoi and Haiphong, or in B-52 strikes on the neutral countries of Cambodia and Laos. The mechanics that concerned me were those of Frost and Nixon. Once into factual questioning on foreign policy, Nixon began, predictably, to assert a complete dominance over Frost. To double-check my instinct, I slipped a transcript of the first three days' sessions to Fawn Brodie, and she wrote me a memorandum in return:

"There is some very good material in the first eighty pages," she wrote, "but what really appalls me is the material that follows the [first day's session]. Here Nixon is on sure ground. He has written, and his staff has written, all of this in his memoirs. He knows his way around the material with confidence. His command over Frost is practically total, which is not true of the first day's taping. It showed Nixon to be vulnerable, garrulous, hesitant, troubled. The taping on Vietnam shows the old master at work.

"If David Frost uses massive material from the Vietnam taping, he will simply be giving the American public an advance look at Nixon's book. Does Frost want to do this? Why should he pay Nixon $600,000 to give us an advance briefing of his incredible defense of the Vietnam War, most of which was written by his staff?"

Fawn found Nixon's laying-off on Kennedy and Johnson in the Vietnam section particularly atrocious. Nixon had said on

the second taping day, "You talked about how do I feel as a
Quaker about [the war]? I hate all of it. I mean, I hate the war;
I hated every minute of it . . . believe me, it was a sore tempta-
tion not just to end it and blame it on Kennedy and Johnson.
They got us in, I didn't. They sent the men over there, I
didn't."

Fawn felt the American audience should be reminded of
three things:

1. Nixon continued to draft men and sent them to
   Vietnam as replacements all through his Administration,
   almost to the signing of the peace treaty.
2. The White House tapes showed Nixon saying to his aides
   about the carpet-bombing, "Try and get the weather,
   damn it, and if any of you know any prayers, say them.
   Let's get the weather cleared up. The bastards have never
   been bombed like they're going to be bombed this time."
3. Nixon ordered the dropping of more bombs than any
   man in history.

Newspapermen, Fawn Brodie wrote me, can never properly set the record as straight as David Frost can now.

But I was at sea. I was not supposed to be farming out transcripts. Had the ever-suspicious Mr. Birt found out, vigilant
as he always was to catch me in some mischief, I would have
been drummed out of the Beverly Hilton. I didn't want that.
I was enjoying myself. The transcripts were guarded, to the

point of paranoia, in the safes in our hotel rooms. And yet when I made these Fawn Brodie arguments as if they were my own, the words sounded, even to my ears, disappointingly dogmatic. The date-by-date emphasis on the mechanics of diplomacy made the carpet-bombing sound like an eminently reasonable course, given the intransigence of the North Vietnamese at the conference table. One had to listen very carefully to discover that Nixon's argument was like the brute in a rape case who pleads that he just couldn't control his masculine impulses. "Yours from the waist up," a novelist friend of mine had signed a letter to Nixon during the devastation of Hanoi and Haiphong.

Earlier, David Frost had demonstrated his superb ability to work well with his staff, and now, attentive to my discomfort over the way the Vietnam questioning was going, he demonstrated it once again. He sent me off to come up with "dream Vietnam questions . . . questions that your radical friends would love to hear asked." Instinctively, I wanted the themes of the Nuremberg Accords treated, and I checked in with several people, including Marcel Ophuls, the producer of *The Memory of Justice,* and Richard Falk, the Princeton historian who had been so active as an intellectual dissident during the war. Ophuls was dismissive and did not want to get involved. He did not envy Frost's role, didn't think one could plan ahead for a good interview, and did not expect Frost's effort to bear fruit. Falk was more helpful, and with him I devised four dream questions. Two are worth noting. In the second session, March 25, 1977, Nixon had clearly prepared a little package on the Lieutenant Calley–My Lai case, comparing that atrocity, as one might expect, with the massacre of 5,000 civilians in Hue during the Tet offensive, and 45,000 civilians in the May offensive of 1972. (Those figures have been shown by subsequent investigation to be way out of line, but Frost did not challenge them.) Nixon's package was inserted in response to a question that had nothing to do with Calley, and it was in situations like that that his preparation was so transparent. Anyway, as a follow-up, I urged David to ask if Nixon accepted the responsibility of civilian and political leadership for military misconduct in war. I urged that Nixon be quoted the opening statement of Associate Justice Robert Jackson, chief prosecutor at Nuremberg:

"If certain acts in violation of treaties are crimes, they are crimes whether the U.S. does them, or whether Germany does them, and we are not prepared to lay down a code of criminal conduct against others which we would be unwilling to invoke against ourselves."

Second, I wanted the "bloodbath" justification for prolonging the war for four years examined. Nixon had repeatedly used the argument that thousands, perhaps millions, of South Vietnamese would be slaughtered as retaliation by North Vietnamese conquerors if the United States pulled out. After defeat, of course, there had been no bloodbath. But Bob Zelnick quashed the questions in his "area," saying that in the case of bloodbath, Nixon would simply counter with statistics on the Cambodian bloodbath that did take place after the Communist takeover there. Apparently, Zelnick did not feel he even had to attack my Nuremberg line. Of course, the dream questions were not asked, but I had been kept busy. With that nostalgic sixties notion of individual witness, I felt better. From the standpoint of my own conscience, I had at least put the information in Frost's hands.

Without any serious challenge, the Vietnam segment ended, predictably enough, on a mawkish note, with Nixon proclaiming, "I was perhaps the last casualty of Vietnam." I was appalled, but David was quite proud of eliciting this astonishing pronouncement. When the foreign policy interview was aired several months later, the brilliant *Los Angeles Times* cartoonist Paul Conrad sketched a Vietnam veteran paraplegic in a wheelchair watching this statement on television with his head buried in his hands.

The days that followed, on SALT, Soviet relations, Mideast negotiations, largely went over my head. I was talking to members of the crew, however, and was receiving the distressing signal that not only was Nixon impressively exercising his control over both the material and Frost, but, bored as they were by the fineries of foreign policy, the crew members might even consider voting for Nixon again if they had the chance. I did not see why these technicians were not a fair barometer of the vast American audience who would watch the programs. We were dealing here not only with substance, but with appearance as well. Indeed, in this forum, appearance was more important than substance. To date, the Old Master was serving himself very nicely.

I began to live for the moments of tension or humor or humanity. Two such moments stick in my mind. The first came in a segment on Chile, where Frost was pressing Nixon on his support of right-wing factions, which were working to defeat President Salvador Allende. As if to clinch his point about the importance of keeping Chile out of Communist hands, Nixon quoted an Italian businessman who made a visit to the White House during the Chilean turmoil.

"If Allende should win the election in Chile, with Castro in Cuba, you will in effect have a Red sandwich in Latin America, and soon it will all be Red," said Nixon's Italian.

"But that's madness of him to say that," said an astonished Frost.

"It's not madness at all. It shows somebody cutting through the hypocritical double standard of those who can see all the dangers on the right, and don't look at the dangers on the left."

But Frost kept with the analogy: these two thin slices of bread many thousands of miles apart, and this enormous hunk of beefy Brazil and Venezuela in between, and suddenly Nixon's law about the hunk of beef in between turning Red looked rather ridiculous. It was an example of a good interviewer sticking to the meaning of words, and not allowing a politician to escape with sloppy conventionality.

The second moment of interest, especially for me, related

to an incident in Ottawa after Nixon's resignation, when Henry Kissinger had been at a state dinner. Seated next to the Canadian defense minister, Kissinger was asked about Nixon and replied that the ex-president was an "odd, unpleasant, and artificial man." The story got out into the newspapers because a microphone in front of Kissinger somehow had been left on. I had checked the details of the story with an Ottawa newspaper, but the question was, how on earth could Frost get into the delicate subject with Nixon? He did it deftly.

"Several years ago Dustin made a movie called *Who Is Harry Kellerman and Why Is He Saying Those Awful Things About Me?* Like the Ottawa banquet—did you sometimes feel, 'Why is Henry Kissinger saying all those terrible things about me?' "

Nixon rolled his eyes to the ceiling. He talked about Kissinger's desire to please, about his love for Hollywood parties, before he volunteered the substance of the Ottawa story.

"He goes to a party, and I can see exactly what happened in Canada. He runs into a lady who has a very low opinion of me, so Henry feels he's really defending me and that the way to defend me is to concede that 'I'm sort of an odd person, I'm an artificial person.' The only problem was, he didn't think to turn the microphone off. But on the other hand, I didn't turn it off either in the Oval Office on occasions."

I commented to David later that he might think about a similar deft entry into the world of Rebozo, Abplanalp, and Nixon, and their games with mannequin legs on Rebozo's yacht. David was noncommittal.

As Nixon asserted his dominance in the fourteen hours (out of twenty-four hours available) of questioning, his chitchat at the beginning and at the end of the taping turned more and more to his strange billingsgate, without the deletions. He told of how his butler, Manolo, would arrive every morning early with the coffee and the presidential china. Now, Manolo was a lover of dogs, and he preferred the Spanish slur "son of a whore" to the English "son of a bitch." "Manolo hates to slander a dog," said the boss. (We were paying for this drivel, I thought to myself.) He commented on Frost's pointed Italian shoes and allowed that on himself they would look effeminate, but then "you're in show business." He told of joking with Mao about the women of Paris (I wondered how either knew), and he allowed that Brezhnev had a very "earthy sense of humor."

Frost didn't have to ask for an example. Brezhnev told the joke at his dacha about the sixty-year-old man who went to his doctor complaining that he could have intercourse only rarely with his wife. That's perfectly normal, the doctor counseled, the man was getting up there in age. Yes, replied the patient, but a sixty-three-year-old friend of mine down the block says he has intercourse with his wife three times a week. "Don't worry," said Nixon's Brezhnev, "you can talk that way, too."

Always one to want his subject at ease, and perhaps never wanting to be upstaged as well, David would occasionally counter with Blue Angel bawdy-house lines on the same level, such as the lawyer Henry Scrotum, whom everyone was always pushing to become a judge, so that he could become a hanging judge. Nixon didn't seem to get it. In the times when Nixon swore on camera, like the time he talked about Ralph Abernathy "pissing on the presidency," it seemed quite deliberate, as if to show how harmless all those expletives deleted from the tapes really were. But somehow all of it, on camera and off, was out of sync. "It would have been damn blackmail," he said once on camera. "I hate the son of a bitch's guts," he said another time.

Into the third week of taping, Nixon took notice of how I always stood silently on the edge of the worker bees who swarmed around him before and after the taping. He began to refer to me as "the quiet one" and then as "the thinker." Once, as he was passing through the kitchen on the way to the set, I said jovially that during one of these sessions, while he and David talked, I was going to join the surfers on the beach below us, who were constantly catching beautifully shaped six-foot waves. Nixon was very interested that I surfed.

"We have the best surfing beach on this whole coastline, off the [San Clemente] complex," he said. "You ought to come down and surf there, and afterward you can come and use our showers." I thanked him. I wasn't sure I would trust a Nixon shower.

. . .

By early April, I had come to view the interviews as an electrical wire through which, except for a little Frost-provided juice over Cambodia and Vietnam, had been whining an idle current for fourteen hours. This now included half hours of dedicated Italian, French, British, and, God forbid, Australian material. (Much of the Australian half hour was spent in a discussion of a dress, slit up the side to the waist, that the Australian prime minister's wife had once worn to a White House state dinner. "She has nice gams," Nixon said complimentarily off camera.) On April 4, at long last, the discussion moved from foreign policy to domestic affairs, and on April 6, the last taping day before Watergate, we came to the most crucial relay point so far: the Huston Plan. This plan, admitted by its author to be illegal, for governmental mail openings, burglaries, wiretaps, and intensified surveillance of college students, is arguably the most anti-democratic document in American history. It was a blueprint to undermine the fundamental right of dissent and free speech in America. As Philip Lacovara, the former special prosecutor, had told me in Washington, it was surprising that the author of the plan was not taken out and summarily shot. Not only was Tom Charles Huston not shot, the plan was calmly considered and signed by Nixon, and was in force for a week, until J. Edgar Hoover objected on territorial rather than philosophical grounds. Only then was approval rescinded (although many felt it remained in effect under the code name COINTELPRO). As the juice gang, Bob Zelnick and I felt Nixon had to be zapped here. If not here, then no place.

The morning began ominously. As we anticipated, Nixon harped on mad bombers like the Weathermen and the Black Panthers. He stressed the 3,000 bombings and 35,000 assaults on police officers in 1971, and he was allowed to paint a picture of America in revolution—without challenge from Frost about the essential nonviolence of war protest. To such an uncontrolled revolutionary America, the Huston Plan was beginning to sound like a rational remedy.

Were there no checks on the President's power to do whatever he wanted, even if it was illegal? Could he do anything, regardless of the law? Burglary? Forgery? Even murder? I had urged Frost to follow this line—one that Senator Herman Talmadge had used with John Ehrlichman during the Ervin hearings.

"If the President does it, that means it's not illegal," Nixon said, almost cavalierly. Never had his imperialism been so baldly stated. So the dividing line between, say, a police burglary and the murder of a dissenter was only the President's judgment? Nixon agreed.

Frost often had the subtlety and restraint to allow Nixon to sink himself, but here the opposing view had to be expressed. How else would the audience know how grotesque, how un-American this answer was? And there were the critics to keep in mind, with "their pencils all sharpened," as John Birt put it, ready to ridicule a weak Frost performance, ready to recite a litany of times that Frost had let Nixon get away with, well, murder. Bob Zelnick was furious, more furious than I, for I felt that Nixon's admission was sufficient. In retrospect, I had become satisfied with partial victory. As an oral adviser, particularly late in the tapings, when the stakes were highest, Zelnick could be superb. In a break before lunch, he came down brutally on Frost.

"You sound like two old chums, sitting around a pork barrel, talking about a bowling game, rather than about the incredible divisiveness that Nixon himself deliberately caused."

"But he's admitted what we wanted him to," David replied lamely, clearly shaken.

"But how is the audience to know?" Bob responded hotly. "You have to state the opposite view."

"Sniping at him is not good enough anymore," Birt added. "The absurdity of his position must be underlined. If you don't respond to the absurdity, then it appears as if you not only accept his view, but endorse it."

After lunch, David went back over some crucial points in a more challenging fashion, and the result was that in the mind of many intelligent viewers later, the portion on the Huston Plan was the most damaging period in all the Nixon interviews. But it had been a fix-it job, and that night, back in the Hilton, Frost's staff continued its barrage. There was now a week's break before the Watergate sessions. Was

David up to this? Would he buckle down and master the material? Could he adopt a disciplined plan for the Watergate show and stick to it? Hours had been devoted to such exotic topics as the Indo-Pakistan conflict and SALT II. We were left with only four hours for the entire Watergate cover-up. Would he be able to deny himself the pleasure of his Hollywood friends for a week? While there had been golden moments here and there in the tapings so far, the Watergate interrogation had to be solid gold. Otherwise the series was dead—commercially as well as substantively. Did Frost realize the jeopardy we were now in? Worse than that: if Nixon's guilt and his authoritarian impulses were not clearly demonstrated, Frost would take an equivalent position in the history of television to that of Nixon in the history of politics. The epitaph would read: *He paid $1 million for Nixon's resurrection.*

That night there was a splendid birthday party for David, a warm celebration of a man for whom many held genuine affection. David's funny and charming playmate, Caroline Cushing (she had inspired Neil Diamond to write "Sweet Caroline"), had arranged a party at Ma Maison in Hollywood. Beef Wellington, sugar-covered strawberries, and two wines festooned the sumptuous menu, while Sammy Cahn, the noted songwriter ("Come Fly with Me," "The September of My Years," "My Kind of Town") provided the entertainment. I renewed my friendship with Michael York, the actor with whom I had been in college at Oxford. Neil Diamond was there, but Dinah Shore had had to cancel. After dinner,

Sammy Cahn sang delightful adaptations of his songs in celebration of David. One of them seemed to have a sobering effect. With his irrepressible grainy voice, Cahn put different lyrics to his old standard, "Love and Marriage":

> *Frost and Nixon, Frost and Nixon,*
> *Now, there's an act that's gonna take some fixin'. . . .*

The next morning David Frost buckled down to work, and went eighteen hours a day for the next six days.

PART III

The Ambush

*All the morning we waited with steadfast heart, and the
seals came forth from the sea in throngs. These then laid
them down in rows along the shore of the sea, and at noon
the old man Proteus came forth from the sea and found the
fatted seals; and he went over all and counted their number. Among the creatures he counted us first, nor did his
heart guess that there was guile; and then he too laid him
down. Thereat, we rushed upon him with shout and threw
our arms about him. That old man did not forget his crafty
wiles. Nay, at the first, he turned into a bearded lion, and
then into a serpent, and a leopard, and a huge boat; then
he turned into flowing water, and into a tree, high and
leafy; but we held on unflinchingly with steadfast heart.
At last, that old man, skilled in wizard arts, grew weary.*

The Odyssey,
BOOK IV, LINES 437–461

I N THIS CRITICAL WEEK before the Watergate sessions, I performed a number of miscellaneous tasks between conferences with David. Meanwhile, Bob Zelnick
was bringing his legal background to bear on the Watergate
show. The scope of the interrogation was being narrowed to
approximate a hostile interrogation of a witness on the stand
about his criminal liabilities between June 17, 1972, the day
of the break-in, to April 30, 1973, the day of departure for
Haldeman, Ehrlichman, Dean, and Kleindienst. The loss of
so much time on foreign policy necessitated this narrowing.
But the decision meant that Nixon would never be questioned on such topics as Butterfield's disclosure of the tapes
and the rumors about his loyalties to the CIA, on the Saturday Night Massacre, on the battle in the courts to prevent the
release of the tapes, or on the January 3 and 4 Colson/Nixon
tapes, to which only Leon Jaworski had listened and afterward wrote that they made him lose respect not only for
Nixon the president, but for Nixon the man. (They contained anti-Semitic remarks about Joseph Kraft and Henry
Kissinger.)

Furthermore, the conclusion had been reached that short,
succinct, factual questions would not work, because that
invited filibuster: Instead, David would preface a question
with a series of facts, placing a construction on them adverse
to Nixon, in accordance with the adverse-inference theory.
Thus the audience would see two separate positions and be
able to judge the strength of each. Further, having planned

and written from an attacking position for eight months, I was now to switch my psychology (as much as I could) to the Nixon defense. In this task the minority reports to the House Judiciary Committee became the primary source, for the minority, too, had put together a chronology of "exculpatory" facts, which on paper or in the courtroom could be easily attacked. But this was television—and time was frightfully short. Weak as their case was, this was Proteus we were dealing with, and the follow-ups had to be direct and pointed.

One job I performed in this week was to address what I considered to be the last line of defense: Nixon would say he was simply in the grand tradition of presidential misconduct, something like what apologist Victor Lasky would argue in his book *It Didn't Start with Watergate*. What was our position? How should David argue that Nixon was different in both degree and kind from all his predecessors? "Nixon nearly persuaded the American people that political crime was normal," Jack Anderson had told Fawn Brodie. How were we to deal with that?

Again Brodie steered me right. She put me onto a little-noticed study, fathered by C. Vann Woodward, the eminent Yale historian, and commissioned by the House Impeachment Committee. The study contained a chapter on the alleged abuses of every American president from George Washington on. I later discussed this study with the novelist Renata Adler, who had worked with John Doar as part of the intellectual inner circle in the House Impeachment Committee. She felt that it was sloppy and poorly managed, but she concurred that one paragraph from Woodward's introduction was worth quoting to Nixon when the factual examination was over. The paragraph read:

Heretofore, no president has been proved to be the chief coordinator of the crime and misdemeanor charged against his own administration as a deliberate course of conduct or plan. Heretofore, no president has been held to be the chief personal beneficiary of misconduct in his administration or of measures taken to destroy or cover up evidence of it. Heretofore, the malfeasance and misdemeanor have had no confessed ideological purpose, no constitutionally subversive ends. Heretofore, no president has been accused of extensively subverting and secretly using established government agencies to defame or discredit political opponents and critics, to obstruct justice, to conceal misconduct and protect criminals, or to deprive citizens of their rights and liberties. Heretofore, no president has been accused of creating secret investigative units to engage in covert and unlawful activities against private citizens and their rights.

It turned out not to be needed.

The trip to Monarch Bay on April 13, 1977, had a totally different flavor from any previous trip. David Frost had peaked at the right moment. He was sharp and excited, and blissfully in command of the material. Before, his questions to his advisers had been tentative; now he was confident and focused on the fine points of argument. For much of the trip we discussed the law on obstruction of justice. James Neal's closing argument to the jury in the cover-up trial had impressed Frost. Neal's treatment of motive and intent had been instructive, especially when he had dissected such exotic legalisms as the concepts of corrupt endeavor and foreseeable consequence.

"The law makes it a criminal offense to corrupt or endeavor to obstruct justice," Neal had explained. "Note the word *endeavor.* It is not an element that obstruction actually did occur if there is a corrupt endeavor to obstruct justice. Members of the jury, any obstruction of justice, because it involves injustice, is a serious matter. It is even more serious when it is carried on or participated in by the very people sworn in to high offices to enforce the law." Later, Neal addressed himself to the matter of duration. "Ladies and gentlemen of the jury, it is the corrupt endeavor to obstruct justice that is the offense. If it [justice] is thwarted for two seconds or two minutes or ten minutes or two weeks, as it was, it is irrelevant. It [justice] was thwarted, it was stopped, it was killed in its tracks for two weeks, and that is the obstruction of justice."

Where the June 23, 1972, smoking-gun conversations were the focus, we expected Nixon to argue that his conversation with FBI acting director Patrick Gray on July 6, 1972, proved he was not trying to obstruct justice. ("Pat, you just continue to conduct your aggressive and thorough investigation.") With Neal's argument, the duration of the obstruction was irrelevant, and Frost would be ready. What was the actual language of the statute, David asked. I handed him the statute, which appeared in a Judiciary Committee's Minority Memorandum on Facts and Law. As we passed through the guard post at the Monarch Bay enclave, David read the law.

> Whoever corruptly endeavors to influence, intimidate, or impede . . . any officer of any court of the United States . . . in the discharge of his duty, or obstructs or impedes or endeavors to influence, obstruct or impede the due administration of justice, shall be fined not more than $5,000 or imprisoned for not more than five years, or both.

I was not entirely comfortable with the legalistic conversation on the way down, however. I hoped that the Watergate interrogation would not get mired in obscure legalisms, so that Frost's Watergate became the pleasure of the American Bar Association, the way Frost's Vietnam had been the pleasure of the Wharton School of Diplomacy—and no one else. Still, I recognized that Proteus would likely attempt a legalistic defense, and that, further, the highest star Frost could shoot for would be demonstrating to the jury of American people on television how Nixon should be fined not more than $5,000 or go to jail for five years, or both. Even if David failed in this showing, a Nixon defense on narrow legalisms, without remorse for wrongdoing, would fail on the moral or public-relations level. In conference the night before, David had said, "If he carries on in a legalistic manner, I think on camera I'll lean over to him and say, 'Mr. President, the American people have been waiting for you to level about these matters, and you're blowing it. This may be the last chance you'll ever have.'" This was the Frost I liked.

The actors took their places. The chitchat was more restrained than usual, more talk about which one of them sweated the most under the strong lights (Philip Roth would have been delighted). There were technical problems, crackles in the audio. Nixon hummed a little. I couldn't make out the tune. A sound of a plane drifted in from overhead. They waited for it to pass. Nixon joked that it was CBS. Ten seconds. Five-four-three-two-one.

"Mr. President, to try to review your conduct over the whole Watergate period is a daunting task. With the perspective of three years now, do you feel that you ever obstructed justice or were part of a conspiracy to obstruct justice?"

What followed in the next two hours, that Wednesday, and two more hours on Friday, has been called a television epic. It had all the elements of high drama (and occasionally high comedy). The tension started high and built toward an almost unbearable, climactic breaking point. It pitted a feisty, beautifully informed inquisitor, playing his surprise cards and rehearsed lines masterfully, aware, finally, of his duty as a surrogate prosecutor, aware of the imperative to prove the guilt that all assumed, creatively using the ploys of judicious contempt and reverse patronizing and deadly humor to reduce his intimidating adversary to apology and mawkishness. At last I came to believe the words I had been mouthing half-heartedly for months: that Frost was the best man in the world for this ultimate task, far better than any American journalist on the scene. Proteus was formidable: his reactions to being surprised proved his astounding resources for maneuver and obfuscation. He exhibited, perhaps as never before, his copious credentials as a "virtuoso of deception."

David's opening gambit of asking the broad question, and hoping for the categorical denial, was met by Nixon's promise to answer—at some future point—but, meanwhile, he approved of going through the story factually. Beyond that, Nixon said, it was important to define Watergate. Did he sell ambassadorships, for example? Did he use $1 million in campaign funds to buy San Clemente? (This distortion of the real charge of impropriety about the San Clemente house was classic Nixon.) Did he raise the price of milk so that milk producers would contribute to his campaign? Did he commit fraud in his income taxes? "Watergate means all of the charges that were thrown at me during the period before I left the presidency." There it was on camera: the struggle that had been going on behind the scenes for three weeks, the attempt to squeeze all negative material into the six hours contracted for "Watergate."

Frost wasn't buying. "Yes, we must take Watergate first," he parried. "Watergate, the cover-up, and the events that sprang from that. It would get very, very confusing if we mix these other subjects you mentioned all together."

Confusing, yes. But confusion was Proteus's defense. Clarity was certainly not in his interest.

David began his first factual question by narrating some of the events on the lower echelons during the weekend after the arrest of the burglars, undisputed facts about actions of Haldeman, Strachan, Ehrlichman, and Dean. Nixon was quick to confuse. "You have lumped together a number of charges, and I can't vouch for the accuracy of them," he said. So facts became charges. "What are the sources, would be a question I would have to ask."

Frost did not bite. "My point here is . . ." and he moved right on to Haldeman's state of knowledge when he met with Nixon on June 20, the first working day back at the White House, when they discussed Watergate in the conversation that later was found to have the eighteen-and-a-half-minute gap. Nixon tried patronizing. "I know as a lawyer you always like to put words in the witness's mouth. I know you never tried to do that in these interviews." Frost ignored it.

Given no room for diversion, Nixon began his answer—not with June 20, however, but with a long discourse about how he did not know in advance about the break-in. He cited a statistic that fifty percent of the people believed he authorized the burglary, and attributed the poll result to the "media barrage." Frost let him talk, "mentally editing out" this long preamble. Then, "So we come back to, what did Haldeman tell you during the eighteen-and-a-half-minute gap?" Haldeman's notes read "a PR offensive to top this" and "the need to be on the attack for diversion." But Nixon ignored those notes. He remembered the notes saying to check the EOB to see whether it was bugged. "Obviously, I was concerned about whether or not the other side was bugging us. You ask, why would I be concerned about that? Well, for a very interesting reason. This matter of bugging didn't start with Watergate. Adlai Stevenson, I don't suppose you know . . . back in 19—" Frost cut him off.

"We'll do this story for parallels later. Let's stick to this question."

The plan the night before was to get the contents of the Haldeman conversation only and deal with its erasure later (for the erasure had not been done until a year and a half afterward). But Frost could not contain himself when Nixon moved quickly on to the question of listening to the tapes and complained about how some were of very poor quality and difficult to hear.

"So you understand why people were so suspicious when you nominated Senator [John] Stennis, who, alas, is partially deaf and very old, to verify the authenticity of the tapes," Frost interjected. "If you and Rose Mary Woods could not hear them clearly, Senator Stennis was not an ideal choice."

"He may be very old—" Nixon began.

"And slightly deaf, too," Frost said.

"And he may have some problems in hearing—but, ah, he is very intelligent."

"But hearing is crucial. You've just said so."

"He would have had no problem. I've been in conversations with John Stennis, time and again, and you don't have to raise your voice in the room when he is there. After all, there's an invention called hearing aids. . . ."

It was high comedy, and Frost was making the most of it. Nixon was clearly rattled.

"The danger, to put it mildly," Frost persisted, "would have been that instead of hundreds of unintelligibles, there would have been thousands of unintelligibles. I merely mean, to pick someone with poor hearing to listen to audiotapes would be like choosing cameramen who are partially blind. It's a dubious way to proceed."

"There isn't a man in the Senate who has higher integrity," Nixon protested.

"We have just this one problem. He might not have been able to hear it."

This was immensely amusing when it was happening, but it was also slander. Months after the interviews, I was to encounter Senator Stennis's daughter at a party in South Carolina, and she said her father's hearing had always been perfect, even after he was physically assaulted on the streets of Washington.

But who erased the tape? Only three people could have. The reason no one was indicted for this destruction of evidence, according to Leon Jaworski, was that there were two too many suspects. Nixon disputed it. The Secret Service men also had access to the tapes, he argued. But dirty-minded cops, destroying evidence in the vaults, did not seem very persuasive.

It certainly wasn't presidential aide Stephen Bull, Nixon said. (Bull had offered to take a lie detector test on the question.) And if Rose Mary Woods had erased anything, it was an accident. Not only that, you should see the load of correspondence that came in from experts, Nixon said, speculating on how the eighteen-and-a-half-minute gap might have occurred. Frost kept the essence clearly in his mind: Nixon had to know who did it, and how.

"There are people who write letters to me and accuse me of being a Mongolian," Frost quipped. "So . . . surely . . ."

"Join the club," Nixon said.

Frost continued with the evidence on the five to nine manual erasures on the tape and the inescapable conclusion that the erasures could not have happened by accident. "So you're asking us to take an awful lot on trust, aren't you?"

"All right, let's get away from trust, because I don't ask you or anyone else to take anything on trust."

More pressing. More evidence, and finally the real reason emerged why Nixon could say no more on this matter. He had testified under oath before a grand jury that he had not erased the tape. He had testified that any erasure his secretary performed could not have been deliberate. "A pardon does not cover anything you do after the pardon. I testified under oath, and I swore both to my own noninvolvement and my belief in her nonresponsibility. . . . No charges have been brought against me, and they could do it, if they felt they had any proof."

The so-called bottom line. In the end, he was hiding behind legal jeopardy. One had to be alert to notice when he blustered about how no incident, so insignificant, so benign, had ever been so blown out of proportion to create an appearance of guilt as the eighteen-and-a-half-minute gap. By characterizing the June 20 Haldeman conversation as benign, Nixon presented Frost with the perfect opener to play our first, and most significant, surprise card.

The first Colson card—the conversation later on the same day, June 20, 1972—was the most significant Frost surprise, not because it put Nixon in the conspiracy at the very outset, three days before his enlistment had previously been established, and not because its remarks about "stonewalling" or hiring lawyers "smart enough to have our people delay, avoiding depositions" were so damaging, not because its contents were any more startling than the other surprises to come. The real significance lay in the chemistry of the interview. Here was Frost at the very outset of the Watergate narrative with new and highly damaging material. What else did he have? How many new tapes would he spring? How sure could Nixon be that his old lines of defense would hold?

I watched Nixon's face closely on the monitor as Frost read the excerpts from the June 20 Colson conversation. His jawline seemed to elongate. The corners of his mouth turned down. His eyes seemed more liquid. One could almost see the complicated dials in his head turning feverishly. It was a marvelously expressive face. The range of movement both within the contours of the visage and with the hands was enormous. In the course of the twenty-eight hours, the face took on this cast only five or six times.

"Now, somewhere you were pretty well informed by that conversation, weren't you?" Frost concluded his litany blandly.

Nixon fumbled for a beginning. Yes, he had been informed of Hunt's involvement by the twentieth; sometime, whether on June 20, 21, or 22, he learned of Liddy's involvement. He knew of the Cubans and McCord. Then he toyed with attacking the validity of Frost's quotations.

"You have read here excerpts out of a conversation with Colson. . . ." Then he thought better of it, switched his thrust. "Let me say what my motive was, and that's the important thing. My motive was not to cover up a criminal action, but to be sure that as far as any slip over . . . or should I say slop over, a better word . . . any slop over in a way that would damage innocent people or blow it into political proportions."

The choice between *slip over* and *slop over* never failed to get a laugh from audiences later.

The discussion moved to the day of smoking guns: June 23, 1972, the day the cover-up was set in place. For over half an hour, the two men engaged in close, sustained argument on the Haldeman tapes that drove Nixon from office. Nixon tried diversion briefly. He spoke of the two-hour breakfast meeting with Congressmen Boggs and Ford, and of a two-hour meeting that day on economic affairs.

"I accept your point that you were busy," Frost conceded. Nixon tried to quibble over the definition of a cover-up, and then came to the core of his defense: he did not have a corrupt motive in having the CIA switch off the FBI investigation of the Mexican checks. His motive was pure political containment, and besides, two weeks later, the FBI did investigate in Mexico. As anticipated, he made much of telling FBI director Patrick Gray to move forward with his investigation on July 6.

Later, Jack Brennan, Nixon's number one, would say that the staff had nearly gotten the ex-president to the point of volunteering the illegality of the June 23 actions. But then Nixon had consulted with lawyers, and here was the fruit. But legalism would not wash, and Frost, the show-business personality, was handed the role of explaining the law, almost as if he were a backwater law professor in Criminal Justice 1.

"If I try to rob a bank and fail, that's no defense. I still tried to rob a bank. I would say you tried to obstruct justice and succeeded in that period [June 23–July 6]."

Nixon stopped him. He granted that Frost was performing as the attorney for the prosecution, but probably he had not read the statute on obstruction of justice. The vision of showing the exact language to David not one hour before flashed through my mind.

"Well, I have," Frost exclaimed.

"Oh, I'm sorry. Of course, you probably have read it, but possibly you might have missed it, because when I read it, many years ago . . . perhaps when I was studying law . . . although the statute didn't even exist then, because it's a relatively new statute as you know." Later this painful floundering was called the "most clear-cut researcher's victory one could witness." Once again, Nixon's impulse to patronize had been a fatal mistake.

The debate wore on with more talk about motive and intent, and finally ended on a clear enunciation of the issue.

"Now, after the Gray conversation, the cover-up went on," Frost declared. "You would say that you were not aware of it. I was arguing that you were part of it as a result of the June 23 conversation."

"You're gonna say that I was a part of it as a result of the June 23 conversation?" It was a crucial moment, a moment that took considerable courage for David Frost.

"Yes," he said stoutly.

"After July 6, when I talked to Gray?" Nixon queried.

Frost solidified his position. "I would have said that you joined a conspiracy which you thereafter never left."

"Then we totally disagree on that."

No journalist in America, I concluded, would have had the courage of Frost in that vital moment. But therein lay the failing of American journalism. For Frost here was an advocate. He was far beyond the narrow American definition of "objective journalism."

From July 1972, David Frost leapt into the chronology to March 21, 1973. That Nixon had joined the conspiracy at the outset had been made clear; his implementation of the cover-up on June 23 had been established. Now to his next major line of defense: that he had not known about the cover-up in all its prodigious grandeur until John Dean explained it all to him in the famous "cancer on the presidency" recitation of March 21—after which Howard Hunt's blackmail demand for $125,000 was paid.

"You would say that you first learned of the cover-up on March 21, is that right?" Frost inquired.

Nixon was more cautious now, but perhaps not cautious enough. He was first informed of Hunt's blackmail demand on March 21, he responded. Of course, Hunt had only launched it on March 15. What about the payment of over $400,000 to the Watergate defendants in the eight months previous? We knew we were on circumstantial ground here. Herbert Kalmbach, Nixon's personal lawyer, had handled the task, but I had been advised not to make too much of the Nixon/ Kalmbach relationship. "Personal lawyer" often meant simply that Kalmbach handled such matters as paying the gardener at San Clemente. Frost made a stab at asserting that Nixon must have known about Kalmbach's surreptitious payments. When it bore no fruit, he moved on to the clemency issue.

In January 1973, Howard Hunt was making a formidable bid for clemency in exchange for a guilty plea in court, and only the president could grant such a thing. It was a situation that required the reentry of the Master Conspirator. But the negotiations with Hunt were conducted on a variety of levels, and usually in Company code. It was hard to prove that the coded signal to Hunt—that presidential clemency would be forthcoming if he pled guilty—came directly from Nixon. There were references in a January 8, 1973, conversation with Colson to "vulnerability" that Hunt posed, in contrast to the Cubans, who had no "direct information." ("I don't care if they spend five years in jail," tough Chuck said.) Frost jabbed at the glaring absence of any humanitarian feeling in that statement, but it was jabbing only.

"So March 21 was the first day you learned about an illegal cover-up?" Frost persisted. He was pushing, hoping for the categorical confirmation from Nixon.

"March 21 was the full import. There were smatterings in between from Dean. I had said over and over again, 'No one in the White House is involved,' and Dean kept reassuring me: 'No one over here knew about it.' On March 13, I think he mentioned Gordon Strachan knew. Within three days, he was saying he possibly knew . . . but I think you're correct in saying that [March 21] was when the full picture was laid out."

The card. Card Number Two. Play the card, I was shouting into the monitor. Now was the time.

"In that case, why did you say in such strong terms to Colson on February 14, more than a month before, 'The cover-up is the main ingredient, that's where we gotta cut our losses. My losses are to be cut. The President's losses got to be cut on the cover-up deal.' "

Again that rare elongation of his face betrayed his shock.

"Why did I say that?" He was stalling for a moment to gather his wits. Frost gave him none.

"February 14," he repeated cryptically.

The protean skill was facing its maximum test. Proteus knew to attack, attack for diversion. But he now was surprised for the second time. Why did he say that? Nixon stalled. Because he had been watching the network news, reading the *New York Times* and the *Washington Post* and its famous series by some "unnamed correspondents who have written a best-selling book since." They were all talking about hush money, about clemency, about a cover-up. There was a lot of talk about a cover-up. That was what he was referring to on February 14, and the cover-up, he said, must be avoided at all costs. It was an exquisite lie, a superb time warp. With all else that was going on, no one (including me) recognized it until later. In fact, there was no talk about a presidential cover-up until the burglar James McCord wrote a letter to Judge Sirica on March 19, 1973, claiming that higher-ups were involved. There was no talk of clemency until testimony about it came much later at the Ervin Committee hearings. And while Woodward and Bernstein were active before January, their best scoops were to come after February 1973. But who in the vast audience would have the old chronology well enough fixed to notice?

Frost let it ride. This was no time for quibbles. Rhythm and tension had to be maintained. He played the next card. Colson again, a day earlier, February 13, and they were discussing who among the higher-ups would step forward and take the Watergate rap. Mitchell couldn't do it. How about Magruder? He's perjured himself, hasn't he? Nixon told Colson. "Probably," Colson replied.

"Well, who the hell's gonna step forward and say it, see my point!" Nixon said.

Frost read the excerpts with a restrained timbre in his voice, looking down at his clipboard with its chockablock blue notes. When he finished, he looked up and asked his question with his eyes fixed over Nixon's head. I had the sense that in these tense, dramatic moments, neither man looked directly into the eyes of the other in this intimate, yet so public, forum.

"So you knew about Magruder's perjury as early as February the thirteenth?" Frost asked.

In the question before, Proteus had found his measure: smother with facts, confuse with personalities. So he went on for four minutes, returning to the summer of '72, introducing Clark MacGregor (MacGregor? Magruder? Who knew the difference anymore?). He made a reference to Dean's book. He talked of how Mitchell and Colson hated each other; how Colson and Ehrlichman hated each other. The stream of words meant nothing. Frost ignored them, pressed on with his script.

"There's one very clear, self-contained quote, and I read the whole of this conversation of February the thirteenth, which I don't think ever has been published."

It was a lamentable opening.

"It hasn't been published, you say?!" Nixon perked up.

"No, it's available to anybody who consults the record, but people don't always consult all the records."

"Oh . . . just wondered if we'd seen it," Nixon said almost endearingly.

Frost savored the moment. "I'm sure you have, yes," he said.

He proceeded to quote: "'When I'm speaking about Watergate, though, that's the whole point of the election, this tremendous investigation rests . . . unless one of the seven begins to talk. That's the problem.'" Frost read the quotation slowly, pausing deliberately before the last crucial phrase. Here was show business superimposed on politics at its best. Frost knew how to read his lines. "Now, in that remark, it seems to me that someone running the cover-up couldn't have expressed it more clearly than that, could he?"

Nixon tried to juggle definitions. What do we mean by "one of the seven begins to talk"? he wanted to know. He pleaded that the president had too many hats: commander in chief, head of government, head of his party, and, in this case, chief law-enforcement officer. He complained about Howard Hunt as a "prolific book writer." Frost kept to the point.

"There was a tremendous vested interest in the seven not talking," he asserted.

Nixon tried national security, switching the time frame away from February to March and April. Frost's tone got harsher, got closer to the bone.

"I still think that one has to go contrary to the normal usage of language, of almost ten thousand gangster movies, to interpret this quote [he repeated it] as anything other than some sort of conspiracy to stop Hunt from talking about something damaging."

"You could state your conclusion, and I've stated my views," Nixon said.

"That's fair," Frost replied cheerfully, and dropped it.

How could the tension get any higher? It could. How much more could one pack into one two-hour session? There was to be more. The finale was yet to come. The March 21 conversation lay ahead. As usual, Frost gave Nixon the chance for a voluntary confession. Looking back on the record now and bearing in mind that Hunt's blackmail demand was paid that evening, wouldn't Nixon say that he had, in fact, endorsed or ratified the payment? It was these broad questions at the beginning of each large area for examination that were so important.

A pattern was emerging: Frost general question; Nixon categorical denial; Frost factual evidence showing the denial to be unsupportable.

"No, the record doesn't show that at all. In fact, the record actually is ambiguous," Nixon said. It was a mistake, but as with all the other mistakes, it would take a moment for Frost to jockey himself into position to spring his trap. Nixon raised Ellsberg and the Plumbers. Hunt was a part of all the seamy things the Plumbers had done, and his emotional stability was in question. Nixon raised clemency again, quoting himself. "I said, you can't provide clemency. That would be wrong for sure." (Tampering with that quote had gotten Haldeman convicted on a perjury count.) If clemency was the bottom line, Nixon argued, then providing money didn't make sense.

This was no time for trading individual excerpts. The context of the conversation was the issue. Frost moved to his Lutherian sixteen points. (1) "You could get a million dollars and you could get it in cash." (2) "Your major guy to keep under control is Hunt." (3) "Don't you have to handle Hunt's financial situation . . ." In the back room, this came as a surprise. This was Frost's flourish. I had no idea how long he would go on, even as well as I knew the text of the March 21 conversation. (4) "Get the million bucks, it would seem to me that it would be worthwhile." (5) "That's worth it, and that's buying time." (6) "First, you've got the Hunt problem. That ought to be handled." Why didn't Nixon stop him? Why did he endure it? David Susskind would tell me later that only because Frost was an Englishman did he get away with this. (7) "That's why your immediate thing, you've got no choice with Hunt, but the 120 or whatever it is, right?" (8) "You'd better damn well get that done but fast." (9) "Now who's gonna talk to him? Colson?"

On television this inquisition seemed to go on for an eternity. Nixon wiped his brow. He put his finger to his strained eye, pulling his eyelid down, as if he had a speck. At length, it was over. What possible question could there be?

Nixon pleaded unfairness. "You're doing something there which I am not doing, and I will not do throughout these broadcasts." (He would do precisely the same thing in the next taping session.) "You have every right to . . . you're reading there out of context, out of order. It's no reflection on you. You know it better than anyone else I know, incidentally, and you're doing it very well. But I'm not going to sit here and read this thing back to you. I could have notes. As you know, I've participated in all these broadcasts without a note in front of me. I may have made some mistakes. . . ." That last line got lost in the heat of the moment. It was the first time he had mentioned any mistakes.

Had Frost gone overboard? Was he overplaying his hand? Was this that dangerous, Mike Wallace–like browbeating that would gain Nixon sympathy? Would people say, "What right does this Englishman have to talk to an American ex-president like that?" It was a close call. To be sure, it was sad, even tragic, perhaps pathetic, that the exercise had to be suffered at all.

Nixon hung on to the unfairness gambit. He rested his case on one quote: "Do you ever have any choice with Hunt?" Why hadn't Frost read that in his sixteen points? Why had he left it off, as Jaworski did in his book, or as John Doar did in the Judiciary Committee (he called it the Senate Judiciary Committee)?

The time to end it had come. We had run over our allotted time. One last card, the final Frost exclusive of the heady day. For the last time, he used the special prosecutor's document on "Richard Nixon and the Money."

"I've been through the record," he said. "I want to be totally fair. Let me read you the last quote on the transcripts that I can find on this matter. You said, Why didn't I go to the last one? I thought sixteen points was enough. The last thing in the transcripts I can find was this: You were talking on April 20, recollecting this [March 21] meeting, and you said to Dean and Haldeman that you remembered saying, 'Christ, turn over any cash we got.'"

There was no response. The prosecution rested.

.   .   .

I viewed the television trial of Richard Nixon as a three-set tennis match. The first set was the three weeks after the break-in, when the cover-up was set in place by the

Grand Conspirator, and kept in place by its "linchpin," to use his own phrase, John Dean. The second set was the period of January through March 21, 1973, when the conspiracy had begun to unravel. Our first Watergate session had covered those first two sets, and in my view Frost had won them handily by surprise, by preparation, and by skilled inquisition. There remained the final set: March 21–April 30, 1973, when Nixon indisputably possessed knowledge of criminal activities, and when a president was bound by the Constitution to "take care that the laws be faithfully executed." It was upon the evidence in this period—before the congressmen had the June 23, 1972, conversations—that President Nixon had been impeached by the House Judiciary Committee. Nixon's construction of this period had been delivered to the nation on April 30, 1973:

"As a result, on March 21, I personally assumed responsibility for coordinating intensive new inquiries into the matter, and I personally ordered those conducting the investigations to get all the facts and to report them directly to me, right here in this office. . . . I was determined that we should get to the bottom of the matter, and the truth should be fully brought out—no matter who was involved."

In short, Nixon would argue that perhaps he was slow, perhaps he was even occasionally inept during these six weeks, but, however slowly, however awkwardly, the principals were fired on April 30, and the constitutional process, by his direction, did move forward.

This period concerned me deeply. For a start, it was enormously complicated, with new personalities such as Henry Peterson in the Justice Department entering the picture, and all the other conspirators rushing to protect their own interests. It was not so much a matter of illegal action as of illegal tone and emphasis, and I considered it virtually impossible in the two hours for Watergate that now remained to us for Frost to demonstrate dramatically that Nixon had not acted more or less as he was duty-bound by the Constitution. Most important, surprise was no longer with us. On the basis of previous breezy sessions on foreign policy, Proteus had misjudged the depth of Frost's Watergate knowledge and miscalculated that a stonewall could survive the Englishman's battering. It was not in his character to so miscalculate twice. Furthermore, Frost had used up all but one of his surprise cards in the first day (although Nixon could not know that), and stern bluffing was all that remained. Finally, while our new tapes provided new strokes in the first two sets, the minority position had been worked out to the finest detail for the March 21–April 30 period and had been debated for months in public and private forums. The literature on the period was vast.

From a dramatic standpoint as well, I worried. What dramatic production that had rising action and tension in the first two acts and a dull, inconclusive third act without resolution could survive the critics? For a third act, I preferred that Frost move quickly through the March 21–April 30 period and finish triumphantly with the litany of lies about scandal that Nixon told the country thereafter: Operation Candor and the rest. It was time, I felt, to desert the legal plain while we still dominated it and move to the moral plain; Nixon had violated his public trust. Within the Frost camp, however, I was the only one who felt that way. Frost was supremely confident now. He felt that the evidence of the last set was strong and could be made comprehensive and convincing. As never before in the day between Watergate sessions, I argued the Nixon position intensely from the minority briefs, determined to undermine Frost's tendency to overconfidence. Continually, I heard myself say in conference, "It seems to me that this all comes out in a wash."

What I could not know was the toll that Frost had taken in the first session.

On April 15, we arrived in Monarch Bay on time as usual. But for the first time in the eight taping sessions, Richard Nixon arrived twenty minutes late. We instantly assigned great importance to this. Nixon looked tired and drawn. On the way to the set, he stopped for a little light banter with me, in which he put forward his theory of Woodrow Wilson as a man of thought and Theodore Roosevelt as a man of action. And you are somewhere in between? I suggested amiably. He agreed. Once in place, Nixon made another stab at getting other matters included in the Watergate six hours—this time, Ellsberg and the Plumbers. True to form, Frost mumbled something charming and evasive.

With the tape rolling, a few loose ends needed clearing up on both sides, and Nixon wanted to go back to the hearing problem of "Judge Stennis."

"Let me say, he is a man of integrity, and I'm not gonna sit here and have that man maligned."

The thrust was halfhearted, but it reminded me of many conversations I had had in Washington with people who asked what we would do if Nixon just got up and stomped out. Early on, we had concluded to our own satisfaction that he would submit to any question, no matter how tough or personal. He knew he would be sued for millions if he walked away.

"We weren't maligning," Frost replied. "We were just talking about his hearing. What you're really saying is there's no truth to the rumor that when you picked up the phone and telephoned him and said, 'Senator Stennis, I'd like you to listen to these tapes,' he replied—Frost put his hand to his ear and screwed up his face like an octogenarian Scrooge— " 'Eh, what?' "

That look of stunned astonishment once again crossed Nixon's face. He hadn't gotten it. He thought Frost was serious. Those wheels seemed once again to be spinning furiously, close to overload.

"What did 'eh, what' mean? . . . ah . . . I don't recall the conversation." Four times burned with new tapes, Nixon thought we had yet another tape!

"That's a joke," Frost whispered. It didn't penetrate.

"Let's just understand . . ." Nixon continued, basso profundo. Frost began to laugh. Nixon could not understand why he was laughing. "Senator Ervin . . . certainly proved it. . . ." In the back room Bob Zelnick and I were laughing so hard that we had to be told to quiet down—our cackles might make it onto the sound track, and no laugh track was contemplated. Mr. Smith's abode had for an instant become a bawdy house. Finally, enlightenment passed over the president, and the wide, artificial smile burst across his face. Later I felt sorry for him in this episode. His hope for a Watergate triumph, for rehabilitation and reentry into politics, had faded on Wednesday. Now that Friday was his last chance to salvage something from Watergate, there was nothing funny about what was happening. But the episode demonstrated his stupendous lack of wit.

Within a minute of this hilarious and painful interchange, as Frost was in the midst of a serious recitation of Nixon's instructions to the CIA, there was a loud explosion. WHAM! Gunshot? People rushed out of our room. My eyes were riveted on the monitor. Nixon sat completely composed. He had not blinked. Utter fright and panic covered Frost's face. A television light above had blown. Nixon said something bland and low-key about assassins, as if he were talking about afternoon tea. I was awestruck by this astonishing serenity.

The light man worked furiously to change his bulb and

check his wiring, while the principals stayed in their places, Frost working to compose himself. Back in the questioner's bedroom, producer John Birt scribbled a note to Frost and took it in to him on the set. As David chatted dilatorily, he glanced at Birt's note. It read, "Don't be sadistic. JB."

With the lights back on, the conversation moved back into chapter-and-verse argumentation over various staff reports intended to put out half-truths during the March 21–April 30 period. First, John Dean was sent to Camp David to write his report: "a complete statement, but make it very incomplete." "Don't get all that damn specific," Nixon said. The report should say, "Nobody is involved." It should be "a self-serving goddamn statement." Frost quoted these instructions to their author.

Nixon tried counterattack. "You read a series of statements, and you left out one key statement where I said, 'If it opens doors, it opens doors.' If it opens doors, so be it . . . it opens doors. I would think you would have found that statement. I made it so clearly on the record."

Frost picked up on the analogy. "There were certain doors that you were very happy to have opened . . . doors that led to Mitchell and Magruder, but [regrettably, he mixed his metaphors] you wanted to pull the wagons around the White House . . . and there were certain other doors that you didn't want opened."

"Just a moment. Let's not quibble about that."

"And therefore," Frost persisted, "I thought that remark was not necessarily favorable to you."

"The idea of pulling the wagons around the White House was John Dean's suggestion," Nixon quibbled.

It was vintage Proteus: if there was a line or phrase in his opponent's riposte, however small or irrelevant, that offered the chance for diversion, Nixon would find it. But if he was skillful at evasive action, perhaps he overestimated his skill. Or perhaps it was a slip in concentration a few minutes later when, for the only time I could remember, he got caught in a bold-faced, factual, provable lie. Frost was tangled in detail about the "Dean Report," which the president, Haldeman, and Ehrlichman were so anxious to have, the report that would show nobody in the White House was involved, and therefore catch Dean in an incriminating position if the whole cover-up unraveled. Rather than write such a report at Camp David, Dean had explored his own criminal vulnerabilities and had hired a criminal lawyer. But even after he had returned from Camp David, he continued to jockey with Haldeman as if he were working on the spurious report. In his book, Dean's last reference to the report was this:

"On Saturday morning, April 14, I went to the office to hide, meditate, and go through the motions of working on the Dean Report. By now, even Haldeman knew that the idea of any report from me was hopeless, but we discussed it anyway, and I would simply say I was still working on it."

Frost was questioning Nixon on a conversation with Henry Peterson of the Justice Department two days later, in which Nixon had referred to the Dean Report as if it existed, and had characterized it as "accurate but not full."

"As you say," Frost stated, "there was no such report, so why tell Peterson there was?"

"Just a moment. Dean did write a report, and that's been made public. The report he did write didn't mention any vulnerability or criminality on the part of the President . . . so let's not get away from that fact."

The lapse was dangerous, and Frost saw the opening. "When did you read the Camp David report?"

"When did I read it?" His habit, when he was caught, was always to repeat a question, so as to give himself a moment to think.

"Yeah, 'cause I didn't know you'd read that."

"Oh, well, much later. I just heard that ah . . . that he had written a report . . . ah . . . the . . . that . . . ah . . . he . . . ah . . . ah, considered it to be inadequate."

He was firmly skewered. His face showed it. His gibberish confirmed it.

"Yeah . . . but I didn't know that anybody had seen it," Frost kept on. "I didn't know that he had submitted it to anyone." The note of tentativeness in Frost's response was unfortunate, for it revealed that he was perhaps not entirely certain.

"Well, I received it, I believe, from Ehrlichman, or possibly Haldeman. I did not talk to Dean on the phone during the period that he was at Camp David . . . and ah . . . that ah . . . the progress with regard to how he was coming on his report . . . what sticks in my mind is, it was fifty-six pages. Ah . . . and ah . . . he was having problems with ah . . . writing the report and so forth and so on."

The definiteness of the lie made Frost hesitate. "But Haldeman or Ehrlichman had a copy of the fifty-six pages?" he asked.

"I assume they had. I assume they have . . . I don't know."

For a moment I wished David had forced the issue. I could hear him say, "Let's stop right there and let my Crack Number One call John Dean and find out the truth of this matter." Or better yet, perhaps, this was the one time in the twenty-eight hours when John Dean should have been Nixon's interrogator instead of Frost, the role that Dean so coveted.

But there was no time for such luxuries. The inquisition had to move forward—to the successor of the Dean Report, the Ehrlichman Report, which was to be, in one of the great phrases of Watergate, a "modified, limited hangout," and to the offer of $200,000 in cash to Haldeman and Ehrlichman for legal fees. By March 30, 1973, with Dean back from Camp David empty-handed, Nixon placed his hopes on an Ehrlichman Report, or so he told the nation the following August. "On March 30, I instructed Mr. Ehrlichman to conduct an independent inquiry and bring all the facts to me." But by then he knew Ehrlichman was a prime suspect in the cover-up.

"That's like asking Al Capone for an independent investigation of organized crime in Chicago," Frost said, savoring another gangster analogy, and delivering the line that he had rehearsed with me the night before. "How could one of the prime suspects, even if he was the Pope, conduct an independent inquiry?"

"Just a moment. Ah, when we talk about his being a prime suspect . . ." As I had come to expect, he went on to define, or to confuse, what "prime suspect" meant in plain English. It was as if for him there was no such thing as simple language and common sense, no objective meaning to words.

.　.　.

As I look back on it now and study the transcript of this second Watergate session, the breaking of Richard Nixon started an hour into that Friday meeting. Frost had finished with the Dean and Ehrlichman "Reports" and moved to a summary with a broad, ethical stroke. Therewith, he delivered another rehearsed line. The night before he had asked what the perfect president would have done after John Dean laid out his narrative of the cover-up. Our answer was simple: the perfect president would have called the cops. Now Frost said, "I still don't know why you didn't pick up the phone and tell the cops. When you found out the things that Haldeman and Ehrlichman had done, there is no evidence anywhere of a rebuke, but only of scenarios and excuses."

Nixon asked if he could take his time now to address that question. It was a curious phrase. None of the time belonged to him. He thought it would be useful for Frost (and the viewers?) to know what he felt he was going through at the time. The melancholy in his tone was seductive, different from his customary combativeness, and he was asking permission for the floor, almost childlike. Frost indulged him—for a time.

For five minutes a disjointed peroration droned on about Richard the Isolated and Richard the Victimized. He took snatches of events that had already been covered in great detail and to his great detriment and fashioned them into something innocuous, even tenderhearted, as if he were a loving craftsman turning a gnarled, decaying branch into a decorative objet d'art. He had forgotten, or hoped his audience would forget, what had already been established. He was reaching for the mantle of the wise elder statesman, dropping like acorns the names of great men with whom he had dealt, and great events in which he had been involved. He spoke of the decency of Haldeman, Ehrlichman, and Mitchell, and of how they and their families had been marred for life. He protested his own ignorance of the law. He started sentimentally into the milk case. That was enough.

"Finish your thesis," Frost said icily, to the cheers in the back room. "Yes, finish your thesis. Let me have a pen, by the way, please. If there's anything that occurs to me, because it's a long speech, and I dropped my pen. Not that there's anything yet, because I've got a good memory—but just give me a pen." What chutzpah! I thought.

Indeed, men in the back room had risen to their feet. Take him back to the facts! Yet the protean tone foreshadowed a shift. Was this a preamble? Was he switching gears? Had he finally realized—too late, to be sure—that he had to be forthright, that he could not win, indeed was losing badly on the factual level? Frost seemed to pick up our signals telepathically. He responded with rapid-fire factual questions. What did Nixon understand by the phrase "keeping them on the reservation," another of Watergate's great phrases? Haldeman and Ehrlichman had made it clear that the hush-money payments were not innocent payments for humanitarian reasons—"not with gloves and phone booths." Questions had become declarative statements. Their grinding quality conveyed none of the significance of what was happening.

Nixon seemed to be only half concentrating on these thrusts, as if the rest of his mind was sorting out his new tactic. He should have thought this out earlier, he was realizing. They were at the point in the chronology of firing Haldeman and Ehrlichman, and Nixon was desperate to move from facts to sentiment.

"Sometimes when you come in and have doubts about them [Haldeman and Ehrlichman], you should just can them. I didn't do that. But if I could just take a moment to conclude why I didn't do it. Because maybe our viewers would like to know why."

He paused plaintively. Would Frost break in? Nixon had had his first paragraph. Would Frost permit him a second? The Englishman nodded permission for him to proceed. How tough, how heartrending, how emotional it was to have to fire splendid men who had been so loyal for so many years, who had been with you through so many mountaintop crises, and who now had made "misjudgments." His talent was that of an amateur photographer who always set the shutter speed too low, and then claimed the resulting blurred picture was a work of art—and yet there was nothing amateurish about this. He remembered the wrenching experience of firing presidential assistant Sherman Adams in 1958 when Eisenhower didn't want to do it. (*Time* later proved that someone else had done it, not Nixon. One more item for Fawn Brodie's file of "Unnecessary Lies.") Then he set the scene. Springtime at Camp David, a gorgeous day with no clouds on the mountain, the tulips in bloom. It was beautiful, but not Shangri-la. (Camp David was Shangri-la only when he was there with Brezhnev.) They were at the presidential cabin, Aspen.

"I don't suppose you've ever been at Aspen," he said.

I don't suppose you've ever been to Dinah Shore's house, I could imagine David replying.

First, Haldeman came in, standing as he usually did, "not a dramatic Nazi storm trooper," just a decent, respected, crew-cut guy. The power of suggestion. He knew full well how many Americans thought of Haldeman as Martin Bormann.

No wonder this sequence so enraged Haldeman that he announced immediately after the interviews his intention to tell everything in a book.

Then the bitter Ehrlichman came in, suggesting that Haldeman should go and he should stay. "You know, John, when I went to bed last night, I hoped, I almost prayed I wouldn't wake up this morning," Nixon had told him. It was his first reference to the death wish. But the president did the dirty deed. He cut off one arm, and then the other. His problem, he said, was that he wasn't a good butcher.

I believed it. Later, Ehrlichman would characterize Nixon's tone that day as "smarmy, maudlin rationalization that will be tested and found false," but I doubted that anyone would care very much about testing it. The grotesqueness made superb television. Its contrast to the hostile factual interrogation was stunning, and, more important, sprinkled through it were the words, usually applied to others, of guilt, of apology, of misjudgment and mistake, and even in reference to himself, to how "he screwed up terribly in what was a little thing and became a big thing." Frost had tried to force an admission of guilt earlier by demonstration. Now he tried it by sentimentality.

"Why not go a little farther. . . . That word *mistake* is a trigger word with people," he said softly. "Would you say to clear the air that, for whatever motives, however waylaid by emotion or whatever you were waylaid by, you were part of a cover-up?"

Nixon would not say that. Having brushed against the flame, he returned to his previous safe position, that he was acting as attorney for the defense and would not have made a good prosecutor in the case.

"Take him back onto the coals!" I was shouting at the monitor in the back room. In the other back room, different things were happening. Nixon's people, too, realized that their boss was floundering at a crucial moment. Did they truly want their man to confess, as they manfully insisted later? But how much of a confession? What would be good for the boss to do at this point? Colonel Jack Brennan emerged from his downstairs post and walked onto the set quietly. Behind the camera, as the tape continued to roll, he held up a note, scrawled on a legal pad. Frost saw, "LET'S TALK." Or was it, as someone later contended, "LET HIM TALK"? It did not matter. If the interrogation was relaxed, how forthcoming would Nixon be? Frost thought quickly. A tape change.

"We'll take a break here. We've got to, ah, change tapes, which means a seven-minute break." Did Nixon want to stop now for lunch, or did he prefer to go on? He preferred to continue.

There was a furious bustle. I started out of our room, and suddenly Jack Brennan was pulling me into Nixon's room. He started to talk excitedly about a deal, then caught a glimpse of David walking down the hallway. Grabbing me by the arm, he pulled me along back into our room and shut the door.

"You've brought him to the toughest moment of his life," he said. "He wants to be forthcoming, but you've got to give him a chance."

What was he offering? Would Nixon admit guilt in a criminal conspiracy? No. What about an impeachable offense? I asked, ready once again to settle for the three-fourths of a loaf. No, Brennan said. Nixon saw the two as identical. Again he repeated that the exile staff had been arguing for days that the Boss confess. The discussion carried on heatedly, without resolution. It was unclear what Brennan was offering in return for David's gentleness, except the information that we had come, as we had already divined, to an unexpected climax. Our furtive negotiations ended without resolution.

In reflection on that brief period of negotiation, I have often wondered what Proteus was doing in the master bedroom. Here was a man who had made an ideology out of crisis. If Brennan was right, that he had been brought to the most difficult moment in his life, a moment where no room was left for maneuver around the truth, what was going through his mind? All his training and skill and experience were suddenly useless. In my mind's eye, I saw him either in crumpled dejection gazing at the shag rug, or standing dramatically in front of the large mirror, tracing the sagging lines and caverns of his hangdog face, as I had noticed him doing once. The crises he had written about—Hiss, Eisenhower's death, the Kennedy debates—had been impersonal, political crises. But now a simple, human crossroads presented itself.

Could he admit his demonstrated guilt, express contrition, and apologize? Two years of national agony were reduced to this human moment. Could he conquer his pride and his conceit? Now we were into Greek theater.

They were back in their chairs, discussing a lugubrious topic: the death of his brother, Arthur, from meningitis at the age of seven. "Arthur was a beautiful child. I wrote a story about him once, when I was a very religious young man." Fawn Brodie will be interested in this, I thought. She had been working for months on the rumor that Arthur really died from being hit on the head with a stone, not meningitis. Who threw the stone? she wanted asked. And now, before this difficult task ahead, Arthur penetrated his consciousness. Why? Had Frost put Arthur there intentionally? I would not have been surprised. Tell the truth for Arthur! came the voice of Knute Rockne, or Chief Newman, transformed into a Yorkshireman.

"We're at an extraordinary moment," Frost opened. Then, ever the showman, he tossed his clipboard away onto the coffee table with a clatter of china and glass. It was well that the statuette of dancing figures had not been on the coffee table. "Would you do what the American people yearn to hear—not because they yearn to hear it, but just to tell all—to level? You've explained how you got caught up in this thing. You've explained your motives. I don't want to quibble about any of that. Coming down to sheer substance, would you go further?"

"Well, what would you express?" said Nixon, gesturing with the blade of his hand to Frost.

Every American journalist I have ever known would shrivel at this plea for help, hiding with terror behind the pose of the uninvolved, "objective" interviewer. The question was worthy of Socrates: Frost must lead Nixon to truth and enlightenment. He took up the challenge, haltingly, even inarticulately at first. "My goodness," was his initial, overwhelmed utterance at this "heart-stopping question." Nixon tried to help.

"I've qualified mistakes. I've tried to say how bad they were. I'm trying to forget the difference between mistake and a crime." (The difference was hard to forget, I granted him. One goes to jail for the latter.)

Groping about for a moment, Frost finally locked onto the categories. One, there were more than mistakes. "There was wrongdoing, whether it was a crime or not. Yes, it may have been a crime, too. Two, the power of the presidency was abused. The oath of office was not fulfilled. And, three, the American people were put through two years of agony, and . . . I apologize. I know how difficult it is for anyone, and most of all you, and I think the American people need to hear it. I think that unless you say it, you're going to be haunted for the rest of your life. . . ." The threat at the end seemed unnecessary.

The apology that followed did not come quietly or succinctly, but when it came, it was electrifying. It began characteristically, with a warm-up: telling speechwriter Ray Price to include the President's own resignation along with Haldeman's and Ehrlichman's in the draft of the presidential statement for April 30, 1973 . . ."if you think I ought to." (One had the distinct suspicion that had Price included Nixon's name, the final draft would have announced the resignations of Haldeman, Ehrlichman, and Price.) It proceeded to the customary preamble of the "good things" he had done from April 30 to August 1974. He owed it to history to point them out first, he said grandiosely. He made a halfhearted stab at things he did not do, but dropped that tack quickly. He vented some bitterness (but not much) on his accusers, speaking of a "five-front war," but mentioning only three fronts: the press, and the partisan staffs of the Judiciary Committee and the special prosecutor. He said most of his statements were fundamentally true. He clung to his legal position that he did not commit a crime because he did not have the requisite corrupt motive for the commission of a crime. All this was preamble, aside, caveat, warm-up—statements in which his character and training forced him to wrap the now inexorable confession. We had come to the Yeatsian epiphany: "*Things fall apart; the center cannot hold . . . Surely some revelation is at hand . . .*"

The center had shifted. He had made horrendous mistakes—mistakes not worthy of a president, mistakes that did not meet the standards of excellence that he had dreamed of as a young boy. His basic insecurity surfaced: "I never thought I was going to be president, incidentally. I thought if

I could maybe be justice of the peace, that would be doing pretty well." Most deeply he regretted his statements about the scandal: they were misleading, he said first, and then later, gaining courage and momentum, he said the statements were not true (*false* was not a word in his vocabulary), for they had not gone as far as they should have (a moral verb), and "for all those things I have a very deep regret."

Frost stunned us by offering him an early escape. "You mean you got caught up in a . . . [he could not find the word] and then it snowballed." And Nixon stunned us equally by not leaping at the gift. He proceeded with a cascade of candor. "It's very kind of you to suggest that, 'Well, this fellow drew you into it. Maybe Ehrlichman should have told you this, and Haldeman should have said this, and Mitchell should have done that' . . . but I don't go with the idea that what brought me down was a coup, a conspiracy. I brought myself down. I gave 'em the sword. They stuck it in and twisted it with relish. I guess if I'd been in their position, I'd'a done the same thing."

That would have been enough. But he went on. In the "critical" period after March 21, when he was acting as a lawyer for the defense rather than doing his presidential duty, he did not meet his responsibility; he went to "the edge of the law." "That I came to the edge, I would have to say that a reasonable person could call that a cover-up." A jury of 200 million reasonable people had concluded on the basis of his actions that he had been the center of the conspiracy. This met the standard of guilt in a civil court if not in a criminal one. And so he had let us down.

"I let down my friends. I let down the country. I let down our system of government, and the dreams of all those young people that ought to get into government, but now think it too corrupt."

By August 1974 he was crippled as president, he went on, and could no longer govern, and so (without mention of the June 23 tape) he had voluntarily impeached himself by resigning.

Our jaws were in our laps. So what did his enemies want him to do? Get down on the floor and grovel?

"No. Never. Because I don't believe I should."

What should he say to the American people now? He was interviewing himself now. Should he have resigned earlier? "Well, that forces me to rationalize now and give you a carefully prepared and cropped statement. I didn't expect this question, frankly."

"Nor did I," Frost said meekly.

He went on to describe a tearful meeting with congressmen half an hour before he went on television to resign. It was one more anecdotal way of saying he had suffered enough. Suffering enough is the normal standard for presidential pardon or amnesty, and along the way in this remarkable apology, Nixon did a remarkable thing: he gave a

critique of his own cover-up. This came by way of his protes-
tations of innocence, based on a supposed lack of criminal
motive.

"If I intended to cover up, believe me I'd'a done it. You
know how I coulda done it so easily? I could have done it
immediately after the election simply by giving clemency to
everyone, and the whole thing would have gone away. But I
knew that the next question was 'Why not amnesty for those
who deserted and went to Canada?' That was my major
reason for not moving in this area."

I did not believe for a minute that wholesale clemency
after the 1972 election, before anyone ever suspected higher-
ups, much less a presidential conspiracy, would have made
Watergate evaporate. But if we grant his reasoning, here was
the final revenge of the Vietnam resisters. So repulsive to
Nixon had been the notion of freeing from exile those who
had opposed his war and refused to fight in it that he would
not even save himself if amnesty for Vietnam War resisters
was the price.

So what did it all come down to? "Yep. I let the American
people down, and I have to carry that burden with me the rest
of my life. My political life is over. I will never yet and never
again have an opportunity to serve in any official capacity."

In that statement, I saw the final success of David Frost's
Nixon interviews. The danger that this encounter would lead
to Nixon's rehabilitation had been smothered. His political
and personal corruption had been demonstrated. His person-

ality had been exposed. With recognition, with acknowledgment, with acceptance of his guilt, he was a different man now.

Three weeks earlier, on March 23, 1977, he had said, "As time passed, I felt I might be able in the field closest to my heart work for peace in the world. . . . I haven't been able to do it yet. But in the few years I have left, I will do it." On April 19 that seemed highly unlikely. On March 23, he said, "They say, 'Why don't you just disappear and be a non-person?' Well, it's not in my nature. I don't intend to." On April 19 his personhood, if it could only be established by the public limelight, was likely to take shape only in the publication of his memoirs. And perhaps not even then, for Lyndon Johnson's apologia on Vietnam had been derided by the critics and ignored by the public. For Nixon, the Frost interviews had made a resounding and triumphant defense in print infinitely harder. The beauty of electronic memoirs is that there is somebody to talk back. In short, in March 1977, San Clemente might very well have been Elba, but in April it was St. Helena for certain.

David Frost was drained from his ordeal. "I think, Mr. President, that [the burden you carry] may be a little lighter after what you've said here."

Proteus was realistic. "I doubt it," he replied.

As I watched this apology—and in the many times I have watched it since—I found it thoroughly satisfying. Once his legalistic defense was shattered by the factual inquisition, and once he was placed in the right frame of mind, with Frost sympathetically inviting the long-awaited "cascade of candor," Nixon went as far as he ever would be able within the strictures of his character. The important thing to me was that this apology was not the product of theatrical premeditation. It had been extracted from Nixon after a grueling four-hour battering. His defenses had to be decimated before an authentic apology could happen. It was not another Nixon scenario; it was real and genuinely sincere.

He had underestimated Frost. When he said to the Englishman after it was over, "You outgunned us," there seemed to be genuine respect, almost admiration, rather than bitterness in the comment. It was the old Gospel, according to Chief Newman: "When you lose, get mad, but get mad at yourself, not at the other guy. Get mad at yourself and what you did."

As life does not always conform to the dictates of good literature or good television, the amazing Friday session did not end with the words "I doubt it." There would be yet another tasty twenty minutes of revealing conversation. His penitence was short-lived, as if it was a momentary lapse, an unavoidable tactical retreat, in need of quick reverse. Not a minute after he had accepted responsibility for his own actions, his natural venality reasserted itself. Instead of leaving the conversation on a high note, there he was once again talking about the uncontrollable "hot rods" that Leon Jaworski inherited from Archibald Cox in the Special Prosecutor's Office, hot rods like my advisers, George Frampton, Rick Ben-Veniste, and Philip Lacovara, who were pushing too far, because they hated him for the war. He was quoting his son-in-law Ed Cox about these hot rods he had known as classmates in Harvard Law School. "They're tough. They're smart, but most of all, they hate you with a passion, mostly because of the war. . . . They're going to hound you and harass you for the rest of your life," Cox had told his father-in-law. "And," continued Nixon, "as we conclude this, I can say they have [hounded me], and they will, and I will take it, I hope, like a man."

Of all the things he said in all the hours I watched, this went to the core of my passion and defined why I had leapt at this assignment and had committed myself so totally to its success. In the end, things always came back to the war.

If this sorry blaming robbed the conclusion of any nobility, the tone was to sink even lower into ghoulish depths. Nixon chose this moment to tell his Martha Mitchell story, this moment of all moments. So tasteless and lowbrow was his drivel about this much-maligned, dead woman as "emotionally disturbed" and as the cause of Watergate (John just wasn't minding the store, because of his "Martha problem," he said) that I shudder even now to repeat it. How difficult it is for me to think of any human being as evil. But this story, told publicly at any time—but particularly at this point of epiphany when I presume he hoped that his own admission of guilt and weakness would be taken as sincere, was revolting. The story was told as if he expected to move his audience with his affection for the Mitchell family. But when he mentioned Martha's "sweet, lovely girl," he did not even get her name right. He called her Marni, instead of her true name, Marti—short for Martha. After this story appeared on television, the town of Little Rock decided to erect a monument to Martha Mitchell as a heroine of Watergate.

It did not end there.

"Did you ever consider," Frost suggested, as only he could, "as this dream came to an end, as many people have, ending not only your presidency, but . . . ?"

"My life?" Nixon offered.

"Yes."

"I'm not the suicidal type. I really ought to be. If [I were], I'd have to be like a cat; I'd'a committed suicide a dozen times."

They rose from their chairs. The workers swarmed around them. Someone started clapping, others joined in. John Bryson, the official photographer for the interviews, a crusty Texan who had taken the famous picture of Hemingway kicking a can on an Idaho road, rushed up to Nixon and said, "Mr. President, I want you to know that's the most moving thing I've ever heard." Nixon walked slowly toward the kitchen. After several paces, midway in a sentence, he winced and reached down to his right leg. Brennan caught him under the arm, supporting him, and then helped him out of the room.

My God, I thought, the phlebitis!

·   ·   ·

Of the specifics of the last two sessions after the mind-bending Watergate hours, I have only a hazy recollection. Deliriously happy as I was over the netting of Proteus, I was still overwhelmed with what had not been covered, and my raw resentment at the time, lost in the early sessions, seethed afresh. Now there were only four hours left to cover Ellsberg and the Plumbers, personal taxes (the questionable expenses at San Clemente and Key Biscayne had already been vetoed by John Birt), and the personal questions that might gratuitously be served up as Reston/Brodie specials. Moreover, significant Watergate loose ends dangled. What about Nixon's knowledge of bugging capabilities within the Republican campaign prior to Watergate? How about the reference on the June 23 tape to protecting CIA director Helms from "a hell of a lot"? There had been no formal questioning about the CIA or Howard Hughes or . . . The list was long.

I argued that we should choose topics for the next session that would build on Nixon's confession and apology. Surely he would want to fight harder than ever to avoid the impression that, guilty on Watergate, he was guilty on everything. Why not hold the hostile questioning on Ellsberg and personal taxes, which were sure to put him in a defensive crouch, until we could sympathetically gain more insight into his character? Given his decimation on Friday, might he not be in a giving mood on personal subjects? But as the weekend proceeded, Bob Zelnick not only presented a full package on Ellsberg, but had a number of loose ends of his own on Kissinger, China, Agnew, and other Washington fascinations. It appeared less and less likely that an organized probe of the Nixon character would be undertaken. Furthermore, prodded by Zelnick and Birt, David now held the opinion that the real insights into this complex personality came unwittingly when Nixon freelanced from factual questions. How did he know? He had not tried a series of direct questions. I interpreted the opinion as laziness.

Still, I reworked my personal questions, emphasizing his life in exile, his hopes for his memoirs, his consultations with Dr. Hutschnecker, and his own drive to power, his friendship with Abplanalp and Rebozo, his relationship with his daughter Julie after she had been so used. I wanted him asked about his own ideology of crisis, and his sense of being let down after a defeat. I wanted Frost to plumb his penchant toward dangerous depression, to which he had confessed in his book *Six Crises.* I wanted him asked why was it that people often saw him as insincere, especially when he prefaced statements by saying, "Let me be candid about . . ." or "Let me make this perfectly clear. . . ." But more and more, my eagerness for this line of questioning felt like an exercise in personal witness.

On the morning of Monday, April 18, Ken Khachigian

made his strongest pitch yet that only one hour and eighteen minutes remained for any "Watergate" material, which included, for him, Ellsberg and personal taxes. The president was tired and could get rattled after seventy minutes of close questioning, Khachigian warned, as if that were to us a warning. John Birt urged David to stick to his script, and simply stay on the air for the full two hours without interruption. (At precisely one hour and eighteen minutes, Khachigian walked onto the set and, behind the camera, kept drawing his hand across his throat for David to cut. David ignored the little factotum, of course, and pressed on relentlessly.)

As usual, a clutch of us convened in the kitchen near 10:30 a.m. to wait for the principals to emerge from their dressing rooms. How would Nixon look after the events of Friday? Would he act any differently? These were questions on all our minds, including that of my wife, Denise, who had lived through the preceding three weeks with me, and who was attending that day her only taping session. As usual, shortly after the assistant producer, Don Clark, gave the five-minute signal to each performer, the heavy footsteps were in the hallway. First David appeared, transformed as usual into his star capacity, greeting all effusively. Then Nixon appeared in the kitchen doorway. David was friendly as ever, and asked him if he had had a nice weekend. Nixon nodded, noncommittal.

"And how about you?" the president returned. "Did you drink much?" David's love for Pouilly Fuisse had become a matter of increasing curiosity for Nixon. David chuckled.

"And," said Nixon, "did you fornicate?"

So stunned was the assemblage at this presidential pruri-
ence that, as much as it was discussed later among us, no one,
including David Frost, could remember what he had replied.
For once, Frost's aplomb failed him. What could one reply?
Perhaps, someone suggested later, if David had only begun
describing a tremendous Hollywood orgy, complete with
women of all sizes, shapes, and races, and endless orgasms,
Nixon would have turned on his heel and run away in terror.
It appeared that the fantasy for the weekend had been What
would it be like to be superstud David Frost in Hollywood,
on the weekend after he had broken Richard Nixon?

Nixon moved on to our little circle. Denise was introduced. Nixon mentioned meeting her sister-in-law once in
Moscow when my brother was a correspondent there.
Somehow, inexplicably, this led to a brief discourse on the
comparative potencies of champagne and vodka, and how
when he was at state dinners with Brezhnev, he always
avoided champagne. "It will put you under the table," he
warned. I could not think what to say. Were my parents still
living in that house on Woodley Road in Washington? he
asked me in our quite apparent puzzlement. No, they had
just moved, I stammered.

"I was only there for dinner . . . once," he said. Was the
tone wistful or angry? I could not tell. Later I learned that he
had never darkened my parents' door. Why would he say such
a thing? (In the session that day he talked of how in the sixties

he had never been invited even once to the Kennedy or Johnson White House, whereas he had invited Caroline and John junior along with Jackie Kennedy, to see the rooms where they had lived as children, and on another occasion had invited Rose Kennedy and Lady Bird Johnson. Somehow this discourse on Nixonian generosity fell flat.)

"One thing I'll say about Reston," he said about Dad, "he's fair." A reference on an April 1973 tape crossed my mind: "President: 'Reston lies.'" He took several steps toward the living room and the set, and then he swirled back and pointed arm's length at Denise and me. "Remember, stay away from that champagne. It will put you under the table." All we could do was nod our heads, and then exchange puzzled glances when he was out of sight.

. . .

As we were nearing the end, I wanted, after the final session that day, to drive ten miles down the coast to see the former Western White House, the present Casa Pacifica (or, as it was in the minds of many, the House of Usher). I considered it not only a required visit after my seven-month odyssey with this man, but also my taxpayer's right. Halfway down, along the endless jumble of neon franchise signs, I stopped at a gas station and called Khachigian to invite myself. His voice was hesitant, but grudgingly he gave me the complicated directions to reach the isolated spot. There would be, of course, no signs along the way to guide me. We passed through the unremarkable little town of San Clemente, and without difficulty found the correct overpass across the San Diego Freeway that led to the unguarded, closed gates of the Coast Guard station that adjoined the Nixon home.

My perception merged with fantasies of St. Helena, volcanic ash underfoot, gloomy steep black cliffs that ran down from the heights into the waves. "The chasm above the harbor looks like the gate of hell as one first sees it from a ship; and the traveler fancies that these dark ramparts must have been built by demons. When the voyager lands, the ground crunches softly beneath his feet, for the soil is made of disintegrated lava. He is treading the road of death. Such is the rock of St. Helena, on which this limitless life might have ended like a tragedy of Aeschylus. Instead, the island becomes the stage for a tragi-comedy." So Napoleon's biographer, Emil Ludwig, described it, along with the semaphores that always flew, blue when General Bonaparte was accompanied; yellow when he was alone; and the red flag never flown: he has vanished. Wasn't I being unfair? Surely there is a difference between an emperor and an imperial president. But is there really a difference between their psychologies of exile? It had taken Napoleon some time as well to come to his profound realization: "No one but myself can be blamed for my fall. . . . I have been my own greatest enemy, the cause of my own disastrous fate."

As Khachigian had instructed, I picked up the phone in its lonely kiosk and stated my business to the voice on the other end. The wooden gates opened on wheels mechanically, and an expanse of grass with the ocean behind spread before me. Down a road, bordered on the right with the wall that separated the Coast Guard station from Casa Pacifica, I turned into a parking lot. At the far end, standing beside a sign that read PRESIDENT NIXON'S OFFICE, I noticed Richard Moore talking to someone. The former White House lawyer had flown in to witness the two Watergate sessions, and I suspected that he was the source of Nixon's bad advice to make his defense on obscure legalisms. Moore's performance as the doddering, forgetful old man before the Ervin Committee was one of the more clever testimonies of the entire hearings, but, on the tapes, Nixon had allowed that Moore had always been pretty sharp with him.

With my first glimpse of the presidential complex, my disappointment that the interviews had not been taped there vanished. The two buildings that made up the offices were little more than oversized mobile homes. I passed the golf cart with the fringed canopy and PRESIDENT NIXON written on the side, and opened the door, hoping no doubt to confront Rose Mary Woods transcribing while on the telephone. Instead, a tanned California lovely hustled me into the adjoining building with excessive haste, I thought, and announced that Mr. Khachigian was in conference. Now that I was on their turf, officious self-importance was the strongest reed they had. Khachigian stayed in "conference" for well over a half hour. I imagined him calculating how long he could stall so that I would leave. I dawdled at the framed color pictures on the wall: Mao, Brezhnev, Sadat, and the splendor of the Middle East palaces. Why couldn't an American president have better accommodations, Nixon had complained to an aide after a Middle East visit.

In his Farewell Address on August 9, 1974, in his memorable Orlando speech in October 1973 in which he said "I am not a crook"—indeed, in the Checkers speech—Nixon had proclaimed that he never profited personally from public life. In an early session with Frost, he had admitted that he was now a millionaire, despite his legal costs, and mentioned real estate deals as one reason. (Frost's blood money was another.) Of course, he had bought the Key Biscayne retreat for $125,000 in 1969, had an elaborate hedge system and a replica of the White House fence (costing $71,000) installed, and sold it for over $400,000 in 1976. The Joint Tax Committee had focused on unpaid taxes on the Nixon properties, but the real question, a committee lawyer told me, was reimbursement, not taxes. Why had Nixon not reimbursed the government for GSA (General Services Administration) expenditures that raised the sale price of the property?

I looked out a bay window, across the parking lot, over the wall, and caught a glimpse of the terra-cotta tiles of Casa Pacifica amid the high, spindly palms. I knew I would not get a chance to view the house's heating system or its sewer system, or even the exhaust fan in the fireplace. No welcome guest, I. In planning Nixon's interrogation on borderline expenses on his houses, I had had the advice of Jim Reum, the House Judiciary Committee attorney who was the San Clemente and Key Biscayne expert. Reum had cautioned me against two "issue clouders." First, don't let Frost exaggerate the amounts spent for Nixon's private pleasure. Use the rock-bottom conservative figure established by the Joint Tax Committee: $100,000. In 1969, $66,000 was improperly spent on San Clemente; $25,684 was money spent by the government for Nixon's personal use. Symbolically, to Reum, an exhaust fan was put in the fireplace, and the bill sent to GSA by Herbert Kalmbach. When the director of GSA questioned the expense, the Secret Service was pressured to give a security reason for the fan—something like, presumably, "Do you want to take the responsibility if the president collapses from smoke inhalation one night when he stokes his fire?"

Reum warned us not to let Nixon dismiss all this by stating he would donate San Clemente to the nation when he died. (Be sure to ask if the papers for the gift have been executed, Reum advised.) The questions about improper expenditures were not moot, even if the property would eventually fall into government hands. The donation of the house to the nation was announced only after San Clemente had become a hot political issue in 1973. The Nixons had then enjoyed the improvements for four years. Under Title 18, Section 641, of the Federal Criminal Code ("knowingly retaining converted property of the United States"), a legal framework existed for an essential element of a crime.

But the opportunity for questioning Nixon on all this had slipped away. John Birt and Bob Zelnick opposed it. Still keen to bore in on Nixon's personal corruption, I pushed for it, but halfheartedly. After his Watergate triumph, I knew that Frost no longer had the stomach for cutting-edge issues. The success of his series was now assured, and his sense of his obligation to history was rapidly slipping away.

At length, Khachigian appeared from his meeting of the hangers-on. (I wondered how many of them were keeping diaries.) He gave me a brief, dutiful tour of the patio that had once teemed with press, the doors that had once led to the Haldeman and Ehrlichman suites. Around on the back lawn, as he pointed to the surfing beach Nixon had mentioned to me, Khachigian expressed some hope that the University of Southern California would now set up a Nixon library. But it was still fuzzy what, if any, papers Nixon could deposit there. I began to feel embarrassed. I had seen what I had come for and was anxious to escape. I asked Khachigian where I could get one of his silk ties with the Mickey Mouse emblem on it, and left hurriedly.

On the way back I stopped briefly at the San Clemente Inn to see the "Nixon Museum." A small enclosure in the lobby of the hygienic motel, it consisted primarily of campaign buttons from his races, laid on velvet in glass cases. An amateurish bronze bust conveyed none of the strength or weakness of his remarkable face. In 1970, I knew, Andrew Wyeth had been the guest of honor at a White House dinner, and in his toast, Nixon had commented on a Wyeth portrait he had seen.

"Andy had found something in that painting that I don't see in the mirror. Believe me, that is the kind of man I want to paint me."

I hoped it would happen. The time had come for the sculptors and the painters with Wyeth's skill to capture the essence of this immensely complicated personality. The future would need special Nixon commemoratives, so that what he stood for would be remembered.

I asked the lady at the front desk if there were any Nixon souvenirs. She went into the bar and was gone for a few minutes. When she returned, she handed me a white, finger-smudged matchbook. Its simple gold letters read, THE WESTERN WHITE HOUSE.

AFTERWORD

O N   T H E   L A S T   D A Y of the tapings, the players in this television epic lingered outside the house in Monarch Bay, chatting amiably. Whatever the outcome of the endeavor—commercial success, editorial approval, or disaster—the ordeal was finally over, and everyone was relieved. I knew, of course, that, whatever the project's fate, we had participated in history. There had never been an event like this before, so it was hard to imagine that it could ever happen again. The encounter had brought just the right subject together with just the right interviewer at just the right moment in the evolution of the medium of television, with just the right dramatic elements. And so I tarried next to the principals as they exchanged their last casual words. Some time later, after I had returned to North Carolina and the reverberations of the interviews continued for months to come, I was being called, in *Playboy* no less, Frost's "top gun."

Forty-five million Americans, a full one-third of the American adult population, watched the Watergate broadcast on May 5, 1977. I watched from my living room in the country, surrounded by friends, and filmed by a CBS film crew that had come up from Atlanta. Earlier in the day, I had held a press conference for what I thought would be a quiet affair with local reporters. To my surprise, they flew in from everywhere to hear me reveal the ten-minute break that Frost had given Nixon to collect himself before his famous apology. The edited ninety-minute broadcast we were watching that night contained no suggestion of a break, as if the apology had flowed seamlessly from the withering interrogation that came before it. It seemed to me important for the public, and perhaps even for history, to know about the pause, for it raised the question of whether the apology was authentic or scripted. If scripted by Nixon and his aides in those furtive ten minutes, it could be viewed as insincere. I knew I was stepping "off the reservation." When he heard about my revelation, David Frost was predictably and understandably furious. After his testy call to me at my home on the night of the broadcast, with the CBS crew giving me my close-up, I did not speak to him again for another ten years. It was as if John Birt had been right all along: I could not be controlled.

Of course, the pollsters were at work overnight, and for me, the numbers were the final vindication. According to the Gallup Poll, 72 percent of those who watched believed that Nixon was guilty of obstruction of justice and other impeachable crimes; 69 percent thought he had lied in the interviews; and 75 percent believed there was no place for him in public life. Before the interviews began, Nixon remarked wistfully, "As time passes, I might be able, in the field closest to my heart, to work for peace in the world. I haven't been able to do it yet. But in the few years I have left, I will do it." After the interviews a role for him as an American plenipotentiary seemed highly unlikely. He died in 1994, with this last dream unfulfilled.

In the fall of 1977, I taught a course with the title "Is Nixon a Tragic Figure?" The standards of classical drama or great literature had come to seem more relevant to me than any detail or new fact that might have emerged from the interviews. In all my writing, both in fiction and in factual and historical prose, I have always clung to a principle that Virginia Woolf enunciated in her wonderful essay "The Art of Biography." Great biography, she wrote, does not include every fact of a given life, but only the "fertile facts" or the "creative facts," i.e., facts that reveal character. With the possible exception of Andrew Johnson, Nixon had become the most humiliated figure in American political history. His character was the last mystery of Watergate, infinitely more interesting and more important than whether he had erased eighteen and a half minutes of audio tape. But what had we really revealed about the Nixon personality? Precious little. David Frost had resisted all my efforts to probe that area. That omission remains my greatest disappointment about the interviews.

On the face of it, Nixon's life did have elements of classical tragedy. He was a figure of great prominence who had fallen from a great height to disgrace. The real drama lies in the fall, the humiliation, the exile, and perhaps (one might hope) in the enlightenment. In the first two acts of *Richard II,* Shakespeare emphasizes how poor and weak a king Richard was. His abuses are accepted without complaint. The action rises in the last three acts, as the king's authority is challenged, as the issue of the divine right of kings is pitted against the excesses of intolerable rule. King Richard is pathetically reduced to the lot of a commoner and eventually murdered. One finds some resonance there in the Nixon drama.

But is he really a tragic figure? All such inquiries must begin with Aristotle. The finest form of tragedy, Aristotle writes in the *Poetics,* has a complex plot in which the protagonist, enjoying great reputation or prosperity, passes from happiness into misery. The spectacle of the fall must evoke in the observer both fear and pity and provide for him a catharsis or purgation that is pleasurable and illuminating about the state of man. On the set in California, most of those elements seemed to be satisfied. Certainly, the plot was complex. Of course, Nixon no longer had the capacity to inspire fear, although if we had lost and he had won, the prospect of his resurrection was frightening. The breaking of Richard Nixon was indeed pleasurable to me, as it was to many of the 45 million who watched. Hearing him apologize was a kind of purgation.

But in the end, one felt only pity for him. He had been brought to his apology, indeed, almost forced into it. It had come partly from his hubris in underestimating Frost and his team, partly through an unrelenting assault on the facts, partly through the surprises that were sprung on him, and finally by taking him by the hand and leading him into the nirvana of contrition. None of it had emerged from his own character, from any deep wellspring of goodness. In the Nixon memoir that followed the Frost interviews two years later, he reverted to form. In it there was no one to answer back. It possessed not an ounce of spontaneity and expressed no real regret.

"I wasted time and now doth time waste me," Richard II proclaims in Shakespeare's play. No line in Nixon's confession quite rose to that height. And indeed, as it actually happened on the set, right after his confession, he turned his fury on my generation, the generation of civil rights and Vietnam. It was these young hot rods in the Special Prosecutor's Office and in the congressional committees who had brought him down. And so his apology took on the form of a temporary lapse, before he returned to self-pity and to blaming others.

In tragedy, suffering must have a point, and the result must be understanding. By the standards of classical tragedy, the Nixon performance fails to qualify. His understanding had been fleeting. "When humanity is seen as devoid of dignity and significance," Edith Hamilton writes in *The Greek Way,* "then the spirit of tragedy departs."

After the "top gun" article that appeared in *Playboy* nearly a year following the interviews, I received a letter from, of all people, Charles Colson. The progenitor of Nixon's enemies list (upon which my own father held an honored place), the self-described "evil genius" of the Nixon White House who once famously proclaimed that he would walk over his own grandmother to reelect Nixon, the man who proposed to firebomb the Brookings Institution and to hire thugs to beat up antiwar demonstrators, the great friend of Watergate burglar E. Howard Hunt, was writing to complain about my lack of objectivity. By 1978, of course, he had long since pled guilty for his obstruction of justice and had been released after serving seven months of a one-to-three-year prison sentence. Since his imprisonment, he had come to Jesus.

"Watergate is now history," Colson wrote. "The passions of the era are mercifully subsiding. I am certainly not an objective observer, since I was a participant; but I would hope that those writing now would do so with an honest and objective eye for history, instead of with a continuing obsessive fear over 'the danger that these interviews would provide Nixon with a means of rehabilitation.' That one sentence out of your article maybe, unfortunately, explains a lot of your other interpretations."

I should have felt immensely grateful to Colson. His thuggish conversations with Nixon had given Frost the surprises he needed to assert control over the Watergate interview. "I do appreciate *the degree* to which you were forthcoming with me, for whatever reason," I wrote back, "because the June 20, February 13 and 14 Colson/Nixon talks made the success of the Frost series, all of it, because they undermined Nixon's previously held positions, brought him closer to the truth than ever before, and from the chemical standpoint, made the apology possible. But I had to do considerably more digging after I saw you to make those conversations meaningful."

In fact I felt only contempt. My passion had not subsided, and a plea for objectivity from this conspirator and felon only fired up my anger once again. There was something deeper, however. His letter brought back to mind the remark of Edward Cox to his father-in-law about the hot rods of the Vietnam generation. I had served three years in the army, 1965–68, during the height of the Vietnam War, and then for six years afterward had become a public advocate for universal amnesty for Vietnam war resisters. In mid-February 1973, that issue was prominent in public debate. At that very time, as Colson was managing the hush-money problem for E. Howard Hunt, he was advising the President's men to tough it out with the Ervin Committee and discussing with Nixon how to cut the President's losses on the "cover-up deal." Only a few days later he changed subjects and wrote his disgusting, hypocritical op-ed piece attacking the advocates of amnesty:

"[The war resisters] are not, as some have said, victims of the war—rather they are victims of their own character deficiencies," he wrote. "We shall never vindicate those who deserted their country, for to do so would be to dishonor the two and one half million who served their country with honor."

In these intervening decades, the passions of the Watergate era have subsided. We have all moved on. A year after his historic Nixon interviews, David Frost went soft again, making a deal with NBC for a lighthearted talk show called *Headliners with David Frost,* in which he interviewed the likes of Richard Helms, the former CIA director, sandwiched between chats with the Bee Gees and John Travolta. The show disappeared without a trace after six weeks. And in a statement to the *New York Times* in 1978, he seemed to undermine his own historic accomplishment in the Nixon interviews by saying, "I ended up with more sympathy for Nixon. I don't think he intended to destroy democracy in America." But Frost did get his knighthood in 1993, and we are meant to call him "Sir David" now. John Birt went on to the daunting post as director general of the BBC, to become a well-known public figure in Britain in his own right, and to become Prime Minister Tony Blair's alter ego during Britain's entry into the Iraq war. He, too, got his peerage and is now known in the House of Lords as Baron Birt of Liverpool. After the Nixon interviews, Bob Zelnick landed on his feet as an ABC correspondent at the Pentagon, in Israel and Moscow, before he turned to teaching and to delivering regular conservative commentary on Boston television. I continued to write books.

After Vietnam, America has experienced two more elective wars and September 11, and few people can remember precisely what Watergate was all about. The Huston Plan, the secret wiretaps, the burglaries, the Plumbers Unit, the cover-up—these iconic touchstones seem distant and even trivial by today's standards, in a country mired down by the

Iraq War abroad and the continuing violation of basic civil liberties at home.

And yet it might be argued that the post–September 11 domestic abuses find their origin in Watergate. In 1977 the commentators were shocked when Nixon said about his bur-glaries and wiretaps, "If the President does it, that means it's not illegal." In 2007 the issue has returned with a vengeance. And one can become almost wistful in realizing that the period after Watergate brought an era of reform. A campaign finance law was passed; Congress reasserted its control over intelligence activities; and moral codes were enunciated for public officials. National security, the *New York Times* editorialized after the interviews, was no longer "the magic incantation" that auto-matically paralyzed inquiry. After September 11, the incanta-tion became magic again. And so, people have asked, after the Bush presidency, who will be his David Frost? It is hard to imagine that there will be one.

In 2007 the Nixon interviews have moved from their place in television history and in American political history into the realm of art. They have become the subject of a hit play by Peter Morgan, called *Frost/Nixon*. Nixon has a return engagement in the form of the veteran actor Frank Langella, whose brilliant performance has made him the toast of the theatrical world. The Frost character is pushed by a character who is called Jim Reston, whose anger grows greater as Nixon becomes more human and more endearing. The dra-matic climax of the play comes with the springing of the

Colson trap, and it is riveting theater. Langella's face is distorted and swollen and he begins to sweat. His eyes dart from side to side and to the ceiling, as his words stumble over one another. A huge screen that hovers above the stage magnifies the actor's physical reactions as he is cornered. It was truly like that thirty years ago.

But somehow, as I sat there in the audience reliving a distant but very proud moment in my life, it seemed that the power of the television close-up had become far more important than the power of apology.

APPENDIX

T HE FOLLOWING are excerpts from the Colson/
Nixon conversations I discovered in the Federal Court
House in Washington. For eight months we kept
them secret. Material from these conversations constituted
the core of the surprises that were sprung on Nixon in the
interviews—and those surprises, more than anything else,
assured the success of the Watergate interrogation.

MEETING BETWEEN THE PRESIDENT AND CHARLES
COLSON, June 20, 1972

*This date is three days after the Watergate break-in and three days
before the "smoking gun" conversation. Material from this conversation provided the first and perhaps most important surprise of Frost's
interrogation of Nixon.*

COLSON: Sir.

PRESIDENT: Hi. Now I hope everybody is not going to get
             in a tizzy about the Democratic Committee.

COLSON: A little. It's a little frustrating . . . *disheartening*
             is the right word.

PRESIDENT: Well.

COLSON: Pick up the goddamned *Washington Post* and see that guilt by association.

                    •   •   •

PRESIDENT: Can't rule out the fact it happened.

COLSON: (Unintelligible) family—they knew us.

PRESIDENT: Really.

COLSON: Sickening, you know. They say, "Were you involved in this thing?"

PRESIDENT: Yeah.

COLSON: Do they think I'm that dumb?

                    •   •   •

PRESIDENT: A lot of people think you oughta wiretap.

COLSON: I'm sure most people . . .

PRESIDENT: . . . Knew why the hell we're doing it, and they probably figure they're doing it to us, which they are.

COLSON: Most people figure that political parties spy on one another and that's part of the problem.

PRESIDENT: That's why they hired this guy in the first place to sweep the rooms, didn't they?

COLSON: Yes, sir. Frankly, sir, I haven't got into the ultimate details that we want on this.

 .   .   .

COLSON: Bob [Haldeman] is pulling it all together. Thus far, I think we've done the right things to date.

PRESIDENT: Basically, they are all pretty hard-line guys.

COLSON: Yes, sir.

PRESIDENT: If we are going to have this funny guy take credit for that . . .

COLSON: You mean Hunt?

PRESIDENT: (Unintelligible.)

COLSON: Of course, I can't believe he's involved. He's too smart to do it this way. He's just too damned shrewd (unintelligible), too many sophisticated techniques . . . put it in the ceiling, hell of a lot easier way.

PRESIDENT: It doesn't sound like a skillful job. If we didn't know better, would have thought it was deliberately botched.

 .   .   .

PRESIDENT: We are just going to leave this where it is, with the Cubans. . . .

COLSON: The fact that they had Hunt's name was the most logical thing in the world, because he ran and trained the chief of the brigade that went to the Bay of Pigs.

PRESIDENT: (Unintelligible.)

COLSON: Bill Buckley is his children's godfather. He's a very hard-right, hard-running guy.

PRESIDENT: Bill Buckley's the kind to write the story.

. . .

PRESIDENT: Mistake would be what?

COLSON: Mistake would be to get all of them zeroed in on it.

PRESIDENT: Oh.

COLSON: Make a big case out of it.

PRESIDENT: Oh shit. I couldn't agree more.

COLSON: Go after it day in and day out.

PRESIDENT: Yeah.

COLSON: I'd say the hell with it, believe me.

PRESIDENT: You gotta keep your people all away from it . . . I cop out.

. . .

PRESIDENT: You look at this damn thing now, and it's gonna be forgotten after a while.

COLSON: This will be forgotten. . . .

PRESIDENT: Oh sure, you know who the hell is going to keep it alive. We're gonna have a court case and indeed . . . the difficulty we'll have ahead, we have got to have lawyers smart enough to have our people delay, avoiding depositions, of course. . . .

COLSON: But this is once when you'd like for people to testify. . . .

PRESIDENT: I'd just stay out of it. That's all there is to it.

· · ·

CONVERSATION BETWEEN CHARLES COLSON AND E. HOWARD HUNT, November 1972

After the break-in, the cover-up was put into place in the following two weeks. In September of 1972, $220,000 was paid to the burglars on the promise of silence. But after Nixon's reelection, their ringleader, Colson's old friend E. Howard Hunt, was herein demanding more hush money. His blackmail of the White House was under way.

COLSON: Hello.

HUNT: Hi.

COLSON: How we doin'?

HUNT: About as well as can be expected. How are you?

COLSON: Just about the same . . . Christ . . . trying to hold the pieces together.

HUNT: Congratulations on your victory.

COLSON: I'm sorry that we haven't been celebrating it together with some good champagne and good scotch, but . . .

HUNT: May yet come a time, who knows.

COLSON: It'll come, I assure you. Before you say anything, let me say a couple of things. I don't know what's going on here other than I'm told that everybody's gonna come out all right. That's all I know.

HUNT: Uh-huh.

COLSON: I've deliberately not asked any specific questions.

HUNT: Right.

COLSON: For this reason. I have my own ideas about how things will turn out.

HUNT: Uh-huh.

COLSON: But I'm not worried about 'em, and you shouldn't be. . . . The less details I know of what's going on, in some ways the better.

HUNT: I appreciate that.

COLSON: So I've tried to stay out of asking specific questions, and it's very hard for me to do that for the reason that you're an old and dear friend, and I'm sure that you regret the day I ever recommended you to the White House.

HUNT: Not in the least, Chuck. I'm just sorry that it turned out the way it did.

COLSON: I hope to hell you had nothing to do with it, and I've clung to that belief and have told people that. If you did have anything to do with it, I'm goddamn sure it's because you were doing what you were told to do. . . .

HUNT: That's exactly right.

COLSON: Because you're a loyal soldier . . . for your country.

HUNT: (Laughs.)

•   •   •

HUNT: The reason I called you is because the commitments that were made to all of us at the onset have not been kept. There's a great deal of unease and concern on the part of the seven defendants. There's a great deal of financial expense here that is not covered. What we've been getting has been coming in very minor drips and drabs. We're now reaching a point at which . . .

COLSON: Don't tell me any more.

HUNT: This is a long-haul thing, but stakes are very, very high . . . I thought you would want to know that this thing must not break apart for foolish reasons.

COLSON: Oh no, Christ no . . .

HUNT: While we get third- and fourthhand reassurances, still "the ready" is not available.

COLSON: I follow you. You've told me all I need to know . . . the less I know really about what happened, the more help I can be to you.

HUNT: All right. We've set a deadline now for the close of business on November 25 for the resolutions, the liquidation of everything that's outstanding . . . I'm talking about promises from July and August. We could understand some hesitancy prior to the election, but there doesn't seem to be any of that now. Of course, we're well aware of the upcoming problems of the Senate.

COLSON: That's where it gets hairy as hell.

●   ●   ●

Two months after this conversation, on February 7, 1973, by a vote of 77–0, the U.S. Senate voted to empanel the Senate Select Committee on Presidential Campaign Activities, known as the Ervin Committee.

●   ●   ●

HUNT: I don't want to bore you with what it's been like, but it hasn't been pleasant for any of us.

COLSON: Oh Jesus Christ, I know it. . . .

HUNT: We're protecting the guys who were really responsible. That's a continuing requirement. But at the same time, this is a two-way street.

COLSON: Um-hum.

HUNT: We think that now is the time when some moves should be made, and surely your cheapest commodity is money.

MEETING BETWEEN THE PRESIDENT AND CHARLES COLSON, January 8, 1973

The day before, the trial of the Watergate Seven, including E. Howard Hunt, had begun, presided over by Judge John Sirica. The U.S. Congress has reconvened.

PRESIDENT: I understand Haldeman is after some kid that bugged Gary Hart.

COLSON: Yeah. That's true.

PRESIDENT: But how could that be? Watergate came before McGovern got off the ground, and I didn't know why the hell we bugged McGovern.

COLSON: Remember. That was after the California primary.

In the 1972 campaign for the Democratic nomination, the California primary was the biggest prize. George McGovern defeated Hubert Humphrey and thereby assured himself of the nomination. McGovern's campaign manager in 1972 was the future senator and presidential candidate Gary Hart.

PRESIDENT: Watergate was?

COLSON: Yeah . . .

PRESIDENT: That's the thing about all of this. We didn't get a goddamn thing from any of it that I can see.

COLSON: Well, frankly, they did, but then what they
                mainly used we knew.

PRESIDENT: Well, don't let it get you down.

COLSON: Oh hell no.

PRESIDENT: I know it's tough for all of you. We're just not
                gonna let it get us down. This a battle. It's a
                fight. It's war, and we just fight. We'll cut them
                down one of these days. Don't you agree?

COLSON: I do.

                           .   .   .

PRESIDENT: The sensitive position is Hunt.

COLSON: The others will just tell the truth and prove
                their case. But there is one advantage to it.
                There'll be a hell of a lot of stuff that'll come
                out.

PRESIDENT: Yeah.

COLSON: Some counts will be dropped against Hunt.
                There will be appeals pending in the other
                cases.

PRESIDENT: As long as this trial is going on, the Congress
                will keep its goddamn, cotton-pickin' hands
                off that trial.

COLSON: They will prejudice defendants in this connection. This will delay the Congress getting
to the point where they believe in immuniz-
ing witnesses.

PRESIDENT: First of all, they're going to make the government prove its case, but none of them are
going to testify, isn't that correct?

COLSON: That's correct.

. . .

PRESIDENT: But you know, Chuck, it's something they all
undertook knowing the risks, right?

COLSON: (Unintelligible.)

PRESIDENT: Did they think they'd get caught?

COLSON: No, I don't think that at all.

PRESIDENT: The Democrats would drop it after the election, no?

COLSON: I think they figured that these were all guys
who were CIA.

PRESIDENT: Yeah.

COLSON: And they all were taking orders from people
like [unintelligible] acting on behalf of John
Mitchell.

John Mitchell was Nixon's "law and order" attorney general until he resigned in 1972 to manage the Committee to Reelect the President (CREEP).

PRESIDENT: Mitchell would take care of them.

COLSON: Yeah.

•   •   •

PRESIDENT: The question of clemency ... Hunt's a simple case. I mean, the man's wife is dead, was killed. He's got one child that has ...

COLSON: Brain damage from an automobile accident.

PRESIDENT: We'll build that son of a bitch up like nobody's business. We'll have Buckley write a column and say that he should have clemency, if you've given eighteen years of service.

COLSON: (Unintelligible.)

PRESIDENT: That's what we'll do.

COLSON: He served under Hunt in the CIA.

In 1951 the conservative columnist William F. Buckley, Jr., was recruited into the CIA, trained as a secret agent, and sent to Mexico City, where his boss was E. Howard Hunt.

PRESIDENT: I would have difficulty with some of the others, you know what I mean.

COLSON: The vulnerabilities are difficult.

PRESIDENT: Are they?

COLSON: Yeah.

PRESIDENT: Why?

COLSON: Because Hunt and Liddy did the work. The others didn't know any direct information.

PRESIDENT: I think I agree.

COLSON: See, I don't give a damn if they spend five years in jail. . . . They can't hurt us. Hunt and Liddy: direct meetings and discussions are very incriminating to us.

G. Gordon Liddy was Howard Hunt's cohort in the Watergate break-in. Together they watched the action from across the street.

PRESIDENT: Liddy is pretty tough.

COLSON: Apparently he is one of these guys who's a masochist. He enjoys punishing himself. That's okay, as long as he remains stable. I mean, he's tough.

PRESIDENT: Jesus.

COLSON: They're both good, healthy, right–wing exuberants.

PRESIDENT: This is the last damn fifty miles.

MEETING BETWEEN THE PRESIDENT AND CHARLES COLSON, February 13, 1973

This meeting occurred six days after the U.S. Senate voted to empanel the Ervin Committee. The President and Colson strategize about how to limit exposure of his top assistants to congressional inquiry.

PRESIDENT: You can let them have lower people. Let them have them. But in terms of the people that are direct advisers to the President, you can say they can do it by written interrogatories, by having Ervin and the two counsels conduct interrogatories. But don't go up there on television.

COLSON: Umm–humm.

PRESIDENT: That's a possible compromise.

COLSON: I think it's a good compromise.

PRESIDENT: They may not accept it. I had thought that maybe we ought to just harden and say nobody can go. I'm afraid that gives an appearance of total cover-up, which would bother me a bit. . . . You let them have some others. . . . That's why you can't go. The people who have direct access to the President can't go.

*   *   *

PRESIDENT: Their license is to go after everything in the campaign.

COLSON: Yeah. That's right.

PRESIDENT: That's the problem.

COLSON: That's an area where you don't know where to draw the line. You can't be a little bit pregnant.

PRESIDENT: Well, we'll cross that bridge when we get to it.

COLSON: I think you're right in terms of trying to limit those who have had direct access to you, because that creates a problem.

PRESIDENT: Absolutely . . .

COLSON: The other point is, who did order Watergate? If it's gonna come out in the hearings, for God's sakes, let it out.

PRESIDENT: Step out now?

COLSON: Least get rid of it now. Take our losses.

PRESIDENT: Well, who the hell do you think did this? Mitchell? He can't do it. He'll perjure himself. He won't admit it. Now, that's the problem. Magruder?

COLSON: I know Magruder does.

PRESIDENT: Well, then he's perjured himself, hasn't he?

COLSON: Probably.

PRESIDENT: All right. What'd you say, then? Let's take our losses? Who the hell's gonna step forward and say it? See my point? I'm afraid we can't risk it, Chuck, unless you have somebody in mind.

COLSON: No.

PRESIDENT: Would you suggest Mitchell? . . . Mitchell seems to have stonewalled it up to this point.

COLSON: Mitchell has got one of those marvelous memories. . . . I don't know. . . . I don't remember what was said. . . .

PRESIDENT: I was busy at the time.

COLSON: Yeah. I don't know. . . .

PRESIDENT: That's his point.

COLSON: I haven't seen anything yet related to this whole incident that has not come out one way or another. It's just that slow, painful process of pulling it out piece by piece.

PRESIDENT: I want you to believe me on this, Chuck, although it's just being repetitious.

COLSON: Oh hell.

PRESIDENT: When I'm speaking about Watergate—that's the whole point of the election—this tremendous investigation rests unless one of the seven begins to talk. That's the problem.

. . .

COLSON: In the case of Haldeman, Ehrlichman, and me, the only three you can probably do this with, they should be either written interrogatories or appointive-type things where they list out some highly specific areas. And that's it and not beyond that. If they try to get beyond that, you just stonewall it or you just don't remember something when you have to.

MEETING BETWEEN THE PRESIDENT AND CHARLES COLSON, February 14, 1973, Oval Office

PRESIDENT: How about Mitchell?

COLSON: John has the most marvelous . . .

PRESIDENT: Great stone face.

COLSON: And convenient memory.

PRESIDENT: On this concern about Hunt cracking . . . suppose the judge calls him in. Do you think that Hunt might just say, "Well, I'll tell my whole story." My view is that he won't tell the whole story. My view is that he'd say, "All right. I will tell what it is." Do you think that's what he would tell them?

COLSON: Yes, sir . . .

PRESIDENT: My view is that he would limit the losses. He wouldn't go all the way.

COLSON: No. He would limit the losses . . . I don't think he'll crack. But who knows? I mean, how do you know what goes through the minds of anybody in a situation like this?

PRESIDENT: Right.

COLSON: God only knows.

* * *

COLSON: That's the travesty of the whole damn thing. No one was hurt. It was a stupid thing, dumb. But my God, it isn't like the Hiss trial.

PRESIDENT: I know that.

COLSON: In terms of the consequences publicly, it's just preposterous.

PRESIDENT: (Unintelligible) because Hiss was a traitor. It was a cover-up.

COLSON: Yeah.

PRESIDENT: A cover-up is the main ingredient.

COLSON: That's the problem.

PRESIDENT: That's where we gotta cut our losses. My losses are to be cut. The President's losses got to be cut on the cover-up deal.

TELEPHONE CONVERSATION BETWEEN
THE PRESIDENT AND CHARLES COLSON,
evening, March 21, 1973

This conversation took place on a famous date in the Watergate saga, March 21, the day in which White House counsel John Dean laid out the full details of the cover-up and declared that there was a "cancer on the presidency." David Frost read copious, damning passages of the Dean conversation to Nixon in the interview, and this recitation became the coup de grace of the Frost/Nixon interviews. But he was ready with this Colson conversation as well. Two days before, James McCord, one of the Watergate burglars, wrote a letter to Judge John Sirica, admitting that he and others had committed perjury in their trial and had pled guilty under duress from Dean and John Mitchell. After this date, the cover-up began to unravel.

Howard Hunt, the ringleader of the Watergate burglars, was the White House's main problem, for he was the one demanding the huge amounts of hush money and a promise of clemency. Earlier in the day, Nixon had said to Dean, "Christ, turn over all the cash we got!" a line that Frost used with devastating effect. Because of his prior relationship with Hunt, Colson was the conduit to his old friend.

On the strength of the March 21 conversations, Hunt's blackmail demand was satisfied with another $120,000 in hush money.

COLSON: I think he [Hunt] wanted to be sure that we knew that he wasn't getting off the reservation. He asked me whether I was in communications with you or with Haldeman, and I said yes. He said, "Well, please, be sure they know we're not getting off the reservation. We want to help."

PRESIDENT: Yeah.

COLSON: We need a channel of information. And we need to know the facts.

PRESIDENT: Um-huh.

COLSON: We'll defend the Administration if we know what the facts are.

• • •

PRESIDENT: What's your judgment as to what ought to be done now. There's various discussions about whether a report should be made or something, you know a report to the President, or just hunker down and take it.

COLSON: Well, my feeling, Mr. President, is that, frankly, thus far, you're not being hurt by this at all. This is a Washington story still. That sounds incredible after all this time and all this publicity. . . .

PRESIDENT: Dean has really done a superb job here keeping all the fires out, but he's concerned about what bubbles out, you know.

COLSON: Well, Dean has a problem also, Mr. President. I didn't want to say this to you Monday night. Dean has done a spectacular job. I don't think anybody could do as good a job as John has done. The problem is not what has happened so far—I mean the mystery of Watergate. . . . The thing that worries me is the possibility of somebody charging an obstruction of justice. Subsequent actions would worry me more than anything. That's where John has done all the things that have to be done. But that makes him more of a participant than you would like. He's the fellow who has to coordinate it all. He's got the best privilege, double privilege. But the subsequent developments would be the only ones that would worry me. I don't worry about how Watergate came about. I think that's been milked out.

PRESIDENT: Um-huh.

COLSON:	It will get so goddamn confused. It may be the stuff afterwards. . . .
PRESIDENT:	You mean with regard to the defendants?
COLSON:	Yeah. That's the general area I mean.
PRESIDENT:	Of course . . .
COLSON:	I don't want to burden you with any . . .
PRESIDENT:	That had to be done. (Laughs.)
COLSON:	Yeah. No second thoughts.
PRESIDENT:	Yeah.
COLSON:	The point is that it limits the ability now to stand up.

TELEPHONE CONVERSATION BETWEEN THE PRESIDENT AND CHARLES COLSON, April 12, 1973

After Frost confronted Nixon in the interview with the March 21 Dean conversation, the tone of the television confrontation began to change. Frost relented in his facts-and-dates inquisition, and this softer approach eventually led to Nixon's confession and apology. But Frost was prepared to carry on with the factual interrogation for the period after March 21 if Nixon continued to stonewall. This is the last Colson conversation Frost had in his bag of tricks.

PRESIDENT:	Basically we have to face the fact that Watergate is a very pervasive Washington story.

COLSON:	Uh–huh.
PRESIDENT:	It's a media story, but it hasn't reached the country. Eventually, of course, it will.
COLSON:	That's right.
PRESIDENT:	And we've gotta keep the damn thing in perspective. But it's terribly difficult for people here. Everybody's in the battle, you know, and thinking this is the only story in town. You get out of town, and you find it isn't the only story.
COLSON:	No.
PRESIDENT:	It's a terrible story for those that are in the goddamn thing, isn't that the problem?
COLSON:	Yes, sir. That is the problem. . . . It's hell, let's face it.
PRESIDENT:	This madman judge is . . . (Laughs.)
	A reference to Judge John Sirica, the judge in the trial of the Watergate burglars.
COLSON:	If it weren't for that, it would be a hell of a lot less of a problem, that's for sure.
PRESIDENT:	Here we've done great things. We've got greater things to do, and here they're talking about this goddamned Watergate.

COLSON: I know.

PRESIDENT: That is disgraceful.

.   .   .

COLSON: My view is that we should decide on what the plan ought to be. Everybody follow it, whatever it is.

PRESIDENT: Um-huh.

COLSON: I think that where this Watergate is hurting us, Mr. President, is not with the man in the street. He just doesn't give a damn.

PRESIDENT: It's the elite.

COLSON: It's with the elite, but worse, it's with the party people.

PRESIDENT: That's what I mean. By the elite, I mean the finance contributors and all those assholes.

.   .   .

COLSON: I have to go back to the point I made to you in January. If there was someone involved . . .

PRESIDENT: He ought to come forward.

COLSON: He's gonna be found out.

PRESIDENT: That's right.

COLSON: But in the process it's going to tar things for you. Frankly there'll be other things falling out that are perfectly innocent and harmless, but . . .

PRESIDENT: Hmmm.

COLSON: . . . viewed in the context now, my God, they'll put him up before a firing squad.

PRESIDENT: All the perfectly legitimate but hard-line . . .

COLSON: Right.

PRESIDENT: . . . and campaign activities appear to be espionage or sabotage. Well, God damn it, they're not.

COLSON: That's . . .

PRESIDENT: The point is somebody's got to step up. But who the hell's gonna do that? (Laughs.)

About the Author

James Reston, Jr., is a critically acclaimed writer and historian whose books include *Fragile Innocence, Dogs of God, Warriors of God, The Last Apocalypse,* and *Galileo: A Life.* He lives in Chevy Chase, Maryland, with his family.